Lévi-Strauss Today

An Introduction to Structural Anthropology

Robert Deliège

Translated by Nora Scott

Oxford • New York

English edition
First published in 2004 by
Berg
Editorial offices:
1st Floor, Angel Court, 81 St Clements Street, Oxford, OX4 1AW, UK
838 Broadway, Third Floor, New York, NY 10003-4812, USA

First published in French as
Introduction à l'anthropologie structurale: Lévi-Strauss aujourd'hui
By Éditions du Seuil

This book is supported by the French Ministry for Foreign Affairs, as part of the Burgess programme headed for the French Embassy in London by Institut Français du Royaume-Uni

Published with the assistance of the French Ministry of Culture
– Centre National du Livre

Berg is the imprint of Oxford International Publishers Ltd.

Library of Congress Cataloguing-in-Publication Data
A catalogue record for this book is available from the Library of Congress.

British Library Cataloguing-in-Publication Data
A catalogue record for this book is available from the British Library.

ISBN 1 85973 833 8 (Cloth)
1 85973 838 9 (Paper)

Typeset by Avocet Typeset, Chilton, Aylesbury, Bucks
Printed in the United Kingdom by Biddles Ltd, Guildford and King's Lynn

www.bergpublishers.com

Contents

Part III
Tristes Tropiques

Part IV
Kinship

Part V
Symbolic Classifications

Part VI
Mythology

Part VII
The Impact of Structuralism on Social Anthropology

Introduction

A Monument

One would have to go a long way to find a structuralist anthropologist today. This movement, which held many intellectuals in thrall for decades, has now fallen so far out of fashion that it might seem like one of those eccentricities of a bygone era. Permeating every one of the human sciences, from linguistics to psychology, structuralism* had become somewhat of a discipline in itself. Even Marxism seemed affected by this movement that was, in many respects, more of a metaphysics than a method.

However, the hope of a true science of humankind and society never materialized, but on the contrary turned out to be a mirage. One by one, researchers turned to other avenues, other movements, other *maîtres à penser*. The theoretical debates they had so intently pursued suddenly seemed devoid of interest, and structuralism faded into the history of the social sciences.

The work of Lévi-Strauss is thus no longer in fashion. It is no longer read with the scarcely contained excitement with which it was once greeted. Now that passions have abated, it can be approached with the requisite serenity. And the first thing that can be said is that his is a monumental œuvre deserving of not only our interest but our admiration. In many regards it could be described as baroque, notably because of its gigantic dimensions, not lacking in a certain harmony that

* The asterisk indicates that the word figures in the glossary at the end of the book.

nevertheless seems at times jeopardized by the profusion of detail. It thus stands among the classics of anthropology* and the social sciences. To be sure, the intellectual method it sets out seems somewhat old fashioned, but it involves a way of "thinking" the world and society that remains original. Not only does Lévi-Strauss deserve our attention for having left an indelible stamp on the history of the social sciences, he remains a source of inspiration and figures among the great thinkers of the twentieth century, while his stature continues to be recognized today.

Lévi-Strauss has penned a near plethora of books and articles. Of all living thinkers, he is certainly the one most written about, and countless works have been devoted to him. These range from pure hagiography to the harshest criticism. The present work aims at more serenity and is addressed first of all to students, with a view to familiarizing them with a body of work that is not easy to approach. This is, then, an overview, an outline of the fundamental features, an unbiased account, but one that does not elude the debates his work has always aroused. I will therefore attempt to translate this work into simple language that does not necessarily eliminate its complexity.

Before going on to the foundations of structuralism in anthropology, I will begin by introducing the man. Then I will examine each of the major themes that has marked the thought of Lévi-Strauss, summarizing them without avoiding sometimes critical conclusions: I will therefore talk about such things as kinship*, mythology and "the savage mind". Finally I will discuss the impact of Levi-Strauss' thought on social anthropology.

A Way of Looking at Things

One could well question the legitimacy of looking for consistency in such a vast work. As Edmund Leach aptly pointed out, Lévi-Strauss' brand of structuralism is not a method, it is "a way of looking at things".[1] In this sense it is perhaps as close to metaphysics as it is to anthropology, and it is not by chance that Lévi-Strauss has attracted the attention of philosophers as well as anthropologists.

The field anthropologist will not fail to be disconcerted by Lévi-Strauss' abstract reconstructions. The question arises therefore of whether it is still necessary to spend time on such a work. And more pertinently, does one really need to read Lévi-Strauss when his ideas are no longer in style? Of course I believe that the answer to this question is "yes". First of all, because his work figures among the social science classics, but even more because it proposes an original way of looking at the world, it asks a number of essential questions that no student of the human sciences can avoid.

Structuralism, particularly the Lévistraussian brand, set off a veritable craze, almost a passion. Suddenly everyone was talking about exchange*, cross-cousin* marriage rules, myths* … The world had become a vast system of binary oppositions; everything could be divided into high and low, raw and cooked, east and west. Considerable effort was expended to make structuralism compatible with Marxism. Today nothing remains of this frenzy, perhaps with the exception of a nostalgia for the intellectual discussions. However, there remains a great body of work that, once stripped of the polemics and the exaltation that surrounded it, deserves our attention more than ever.

Notes

1. E. Leach, *Lévi-Strauss*, London, Fontana, 1970, p. 8.

Part I
The Life and Work of Lévi-Strauss

–1–

Some Biographical Elements

A French Intellectual

Of all the living anthropologists, Lévi-Strauss is without doubt the best known and the one who has left the deepest mark on the discipline. If his theoretical positions do not really make headlines today, his prestige and authority are still widely recognized.

Family Background

Claude Lévi-Strauss was born into a family of artists, both musicians and painters. His father was a portrait painter. In 1908, a commission took him, together with his wife, to Brussels, and it was there that their child was born. Shortly after the birth, the family returned to their Parisian home, at 26 rue Poussin. There Lévi-Strauss spent his childhood and adolescence, in an environment that was both intellectually and culturally rich. Materially speaking, however, life was not always easy. We find hints of his upbringing throughout his work, which show a refined taste in music and painting; he would later see artistic production as one of the major expressions of humankind and of the mind. At times he regarded his own works as artistic constructions, and even the "savage" was for him never far removed from the esthete. Yet one sometimes has the impression that for him the *beaux-arts* are more a matter of intellect than of emotion. Or at least that is the way he treats them in his writings. The work of art reveals the mind behind it and is therefore inseparable from the intellect.

Education

Lévi-Strauss' political commitments would be just as intellectual. While he was attending the Janson-de-Sailly *lycée*, a Belgian socialist militant and friend of the family suggested he read Proudhon, and above all Marx. The youth was captivated, and even became an active member of the French Socialist Party for a time. In 1932, he stood for local election, but this engagement was short lived, and as far as his work is concerned his interest in Marxism and socialism was above all intellectual; Lévi-Strauss regarded them simply as systems of thought, never as revolutionary ideologies.

At the Sorbonne, he studied both law and philosophy, which were to lead him to a double *licence*, the competitive *agrégation* examination and a teaching position in the small south-western French town of Mont-de-Marsan. But he soon became bored with teaching and he, who would later admit to detesting travel, was gripped with the desire to see the world; in 1935, with the support of Célestin Bouglé, who had directed his thesis, he obtained a position at the University of São Paolo.

It was at that time that he felt a dawning interest in anthropology, prompted by a taste for exoticism* and adventure. As we will see, there is a hint of romanticism* about his books. He began to read a few texts, but he received no formal training and therefore can be considered to be self taught. As the end of his first year in Brazil, he undertook an "expedition" to Mato Grosso, where he encountered the Caduveo and the Bororo Indians.

First Encounters

These first contacts would never produce any ethnographic studies in the proper sense of the term. From the outset, Lévi-Strauss displayed a taste for material and artistic culture, notably by accumulating a collection of Indian objects that would later be exhibited in Paris. The savage retained his strangeness for Lévi-Strauss, and he would always prefer the philosopher's admiration from afar to the anthropologist's intimacy. For him, the "savage" is more apparent in a mask, in a myth, in other words in something both closed and frozen, than in daily activities. Thus, as we will see later, Lévi-Strauss gives the impression that the principle occupation of indigenous people is of an intellectual order.

In 1936, he organized a second "expedition", this time to the Nambikwara Indians. The little ethnographic material he would publish came from this trip. The rest of his work rests on the compilation of information gathered by others, and, in the recent history of anthropology, Lévi-Strauss is the only one not to have distinguished himself by his qualities as an ethnographer.

New York, Paris

The Second World War broke out shortly after Lévi-Strauss returned to France. He was mobilized and, in the debacle, found himself in the Cévennes region. With his name, there was no question of returning to occupied Paris, and the Rockefeller Foundation gave him a chance to leave for New York, thanks to the help, in particular, of Robert Lowie and Alfred Métraux.

His stay in the United States would definitively discourage him from any further political engagements, and would familiarize him intellectually with American anthropology, or, better, the anthropology of the Americas; it would also whet his appetite for museums and primitive art, and would enable him to turn his back on philosophy for good. While in New York, Lévi-Strauss associated with such well-known figures as André Breton, Alfred Métraux, but especially Roman Jakobson, who introduced him to linguistics and structural analysis. It was at the New York Public Library that Lévi-Strauss undertook an intensive study of the ethnological literature and laid the groundwork for his first volumes. After the Liberation of Paris, and a brief return to France, he obtained a post as cultural attaché in New York, where he would live until the end of 1947 when he returned to France for good.

Return to France

In 1948, Lévi-Strauss defended a thesis at the Sorbonne entitled *Les Structures élémentaires de la parenté*, which was published in book form the following year.[1] This is a truly masterful work of gargantuan proportions, an intellectually ambitious undertaking that immediately sparked the enthusiasm of specialists and the intellectual reading audience alike. It was no doubt one of Lévi-Strauss' great merits to be able to attract a large audience without actually making concessions or yielding to opportunism. Suddenly everyone, from sociologists to philosophers, was reading his work, studying it, discussing it. Thanks to Lévi-Strauss, anthropology, which had until then been confined to a walk-on role on the French intellectual stage, had become a noble and leading discipline. Though it is hard to assess his true impact, he unquestionably inspired a deep fascination; his works were an inexhaustible source of inspiration, and everyone was seized by a passion for rules of exchange, the shift from nature to culture and the structural analysis of myths.

Immediately upon returning to France, Lévi-Strauss began teaching at the Institut d'Ethnologie, and, with the support of Georges Dumézil, was elected to the Ecole Pratique des Hautes Etudes. He also worked for Unesco, attempting to "give the impression that an institution with no purpose and no function had a *raison d'être*". In 1959, after two unsuccessful attempts, he won an appointment to the Collège de France, where he founded the Laboratoire d'Anthropologie Sociale and the journal *L'Homme*, and thus inaugurated the revival of French anthropology. He soon became the most quoted, most respected intellectual in France. Even the turbulent events of May 1968 would not diminish his stature.

The French Academy

His renown, together with his literary and intellectual qualities, led Lévi-Strauss to the French Academy in 1973. He was at the height of his fame. His reputation extended far beyond national borders, and he became a reference for Anglo-Saxon anthropology, usually impervious to outside influences. His works were translated into countless languages; his ideas were discussed throughout the world. Paradoxically, the better part of his work had long since been written, and he would thereafter produce only a few studies of secondary importance.

With Fernand Braudel, he was one of the founders of the Sixth Section of the Ecole Pratique des Hautes Etudes, which in 1974 would become the Ecole des Hautes Etudes en Sciences Sociales. Lévi-Strauss was awarded the Centre National de la Recherche Scientifique Gold Medal, was made doctor *honoris causa* by numerous universities abroad and continues to enjoy considerable prestige, even though the structuralist movement has gradually lost its audience.

–2–

His Work

Kinship and Structural Anthropology

Few anthropologists have written so much and on so many topics. Lévi-Strauss has also been as widely read as written about, and fashion alone cannot account for this interest. It could be said that one of the constants of his work is to have shown that the study of indigenous peoples gives us a better understanding of humankind in general. The publication of *La Vie familiale et sociale des Indiens Nambikwara* did not leave a mark on the history of anthropology, and it is the only one of Lévi-Strauss' books that is no longer in print.[2] However, in 1949 he published one of the most remarkable books to have appeared in the social sciences, *The Elementary Structures of Kinship*. The work is a monumental synthesis of the rules governing cross-cousin marriage. There was to be a second volume, but the project was abandoned, no doubt because it proved to be a dead end.

If this first major work is technical and difficult to approach, the next two address a much wider audience. *Race and History*, published in French and English in 1952, was written at the behest of Unesco. It was a small, fairly general work, and its conventional character did not really augur the originality of its author. Such was not the case of *Tristes Tropiques*, which appeared three years later, and went on to become a veritable classic of travel literature and one of the great books in the French literature of the second half of the twentieth century. It is without a doubt one of Lévi-Strauss' most accessible books and the one that most contributed to his renown.

In 1958, the author returned to more theoretical considerations with the publication of the French edition of *Structural Anthropology*, followed in 1972 by *Structural Anthropology II* and *The View from Afar* in 1985. These three collections of very different texts aimed to lay the foundations of a structural approach to anthropology.

Symbolic Thought

Totemism and *The Savage Mind*, both published originally in 1962, are of a fairly technical nature. This is particularly true of *The Savage Mind*, which was nevertheless much quoted because it addressed problems of a philosophical order. In it the author deals with symbolic classifications* and the relationship between nature and culture.

The four volumes of *Introduction to a Science of Mythology* appeared in French between 1964 and 1971. The enterprise now seems as ambitious as it turned out to be relatively sterile. To be sure, these volumes would make their contribution to their author's fame, but their influence is much more debatable, and reading them leaves one somewhat perplexed; so much of his analysis of myths seems to be difficult to apply, sometimes pedantic and submerged by the profusion of detail. In 1985, a fifth volume, *The Jealous Potter*, completed this gigantic endeavor to analyze the corpus of Amerindian mythology.

Alongside these works were published, in 1961, a long interview with Georges Charbonnier, dealing mainly with art, and, in 1984, *Anthropology and Myth: Lectures, 1951–1982*, a not particularly inspired work based on Lévi-Strauss' lectures at the Collège de France. Without doubt, the event of these most recent decades was the publication of his remarkable conversations with Didier Eribon, *Conversations with Claude Lévi-Strauss* (French edition in 1988), which illuminate the life of Lévi-Strauss while discussing the major themes that have occupied his mind.[3]

An Inexhaustible Source of Inspiration

Many writings, not all of equal value, have been devoted to the work of Lévi-Strauss. Among the most recent we find *Claude Lévi-Strauss*, by Marcel Hénaff. Perhaps the best overview and most original is Dan Sperber's *Le Structuralisme en anthropologie.* For a critical viewpoint, the reader can turn to *Contre l'idéologie structuraliste*, by Henri Lefebvre, or Bernard

Taking a Stand

Lévi-Strauss has never claimed to be an "engaged" intellectual and has never used his public prominence to impose his personal ideals. Nevertheless, he has sometimes not hesitated to take a stand that went against the prevailing ideology. Here, for instance, is his position on racism:

"As an anthropologist, I am convinced that racist theories are both monstrous and absurd. But by trivializing the notion of racism, applying it this way and that, we empty it of its meaning and run the risk of producing a result counter to the one we seek … That cultures, all the while respecting each other, can feel greater or less affinity with certain others, is a factual situation that has always existed. It is the normal course of human conduct. By condemning it as racist, one runs the risk of playing into the enemy's hand, for many naive people will say, if that's racism, then I'm racist."

Or concerning the events of May 1968:

"Once the first moment of curiosity had worn off, once the strangeness had become tiresome, I found May 1968 repugnant … because I can't accept cutting down trees for barricades (trees are life and life is to be respected), turning public places that benefit everyone and are the responsibility of all into trash heaps, or scrawling graffiti on university buildings or elsewhere … For me, May 1968 was symptomatic of yet another step downward in the deterioration of the university, which began a long time ago."[4]

Delfendahl's *Le Clair et l'obscur*. An incalculable number of special issues have been devoted to Lévi-Strauss and his work, among which are those published by the journals *Esprit*, *Les Temps modernes*, *L'Arc*, *La Pensée*, *Les Annales* and *Critique*. In fact most journals in the human sciences, literary criticism, history, philosophy or philology have addressed his work. Even more articles examine a particular aspect of his thought: many of the best-known names in the human sciences and philosophy have thus discussed Lévi-Strauss' ideas, among the most famous of whom are Jean-Paul Sartre, Maurice Merleau-Ponty, Louis Dumont, Clifford Geertz, Ernest Gellner, Jack Goody, François Furet, Algerdas Julien Greimas, Marvin Harris, Jacques Le Goff, Jean Piaget, Marshall Sahlins, Vladimir Propp, Paul Ricœur, to mention only a few. This far from exhaustive list attests to the interest prompted by the writings of Lévi-Strauss. For there is no doubt that no other contemporary author has aroused so much reaction, enthusiasm and criticism.

Notes

1. Published in English in 1969 as *The Elementary Structures of Kinship* (see bibliography).
2. C. Lévi-Stauss, *La Vie familiale et sociale des Indiens Nambikwara*, Paris, Société des Américanistes, 1948.
3. C. Lévi-Strauss, *De près et de loin: entretiens avec Didier Eribon*, Paris, Odile Jacob, 1988, p. 90.
4. C. Lévi-Strauss, *Conversations with Claude Lévi-Strauss*, with Didier Eribon, translated by Paula Wissing, Chicago, University of Chicago Press, 1991, pp. 150 and 80.

Part II
Structuralist Thought

–1–

The Foundations

The life-work of Lévi-Strauss is an eminently original undertaking, a truly unique moment in the history of the social sciences. And yet it also fits within an intellectual tradition. It could be said to constitute an attempt to demonstrate the validity of Rousseau's philosophical intuitions. It is profoundly marked by the French intellectual tradition and yet at the same time open to other schools, while having had an extraordinary influence outside France.

Rousseau, Inventor of the Sciences of Man

In an article in *Structural Anthropology II*, Lévi-Strauss refers to Jean-Jacques Rousseau as the "inventor of the sciences of man", in other words, the first anthropologist, in the broad sense of the term. This is not a gratuitous claim, one might even say that it underlies the whole system of Lévi-Strauss' thought, which sees the "savage" as someone pure, uncorrupted by our laws and capable of teaching us many things about ourselves. Like Rousseau, Lévi-Strauss does not study "savage man" in his own right simply because he has a taste for exoticism, but precisely because he sees the life of "primitive peoples" as a pure, original form of life.

Rousseau regards the savage as a kind of primordial man and affirms the importance of studying men so as to gain a better understanding of Man. He thus formulates what might be the very goal of anthropological studies:

> When one proposes to study men one has to look close by; but in order to study man one has to learn to cast one's glance afar; one has to begin by observing the differences in order to discover the properties.[1]

In identifying Rousseau as the father of anthropology, Lévi-Strauss breaks with Anglo-American empiricism* and more particularly with the Malinowskian brand of epistemology, which formed the basis of participant observation*. For Lévi-Strauss, knowledge does not derive from experience. In *Totemism*, he shows how philosophers like Rousseau and Bergson were more successful in penetrating the meaning of totemic classifications because they did not seek to understand them through the simple observation of concrete manifestations but attuned themselves to the totemic way of thinking.

Finally, in *Tristes Tropiques*, Lévi-Strauss sees anthropology as confirming Rousseau's hypotheses. Lévi-Strauss travels to the ends of the earth in search of the philosopher. Characteristically, each time he finds himself in the presence of natives, Lévi-Strauss harks back to famous thinkers, and more particularly to Rousseau. The contract, he writes, is the raw material of social life, and societies are founded on reciprocity.

Structural Linguistics

The origins of structuralism go back to Ferdinand de Saussure's *Course in General Linguistics*.[2] One of the basic principles of Saussure's work is the distinction between language (*la langue*) and speech (*la parole*). According to Saussure, linguistics must separate language and speech. One is social, the other individual. If linguistics is to become a science, it needs to concentrate on language, that is to say on the social part of language, which is external to the individual, existing outside the speaking subject in the form of a system of signs. In deciding not to study speech, Saussure turns away from the speaking subject, from the actor, in order to concentrate uniquely on a system of signs known as language. The sign is a combination of a concept (the signification) and a sound pattern (the signal).

In considering language as a codified social system, Saussure, and structural linguists in general, expelled individual practices and diachrony from the field of linguistics. Like Saussure, Lévi-Strauss too would turn away from social actors and ongoing change. He would see social life as a system, a set of relations that precede the individual. In this perspective, the subject is reduced to its simplest expression. Likewise, structural analysis does not lend itself to the study of transformations, of change or of social conflict. Thus, as we will see below, primitive societies, which Lévi-Strauss terms "cold societies", have eliminated conflict and entropy (disorder); they form harmonious wholes living by rules and exchange.

Lévi-Strauss admired the progress made by linguistics, the only one of the social sciences able to claim the status of a true science. He wanted to take anthropology down the same road by eliminating the cumbersome thinking, speaking and acting subject. By adopting the linguistic model, social life can be seen as a system of relations that precedes the individual members of society and is subsequently forced on them.

Mauss and Exchange

The French sociologist Marcel Mauss was a third source of inspiration for Lévi-Strauss' thinking. It was above all his essay *The Gift* that was to leave a lasting impression.[3] In this overview, Mauss seeks to uncover the nature of transactions in primitive societies not governed by market forces. Comparing a number of practices found in various parts of the world, Mauss concludes that gift-exchange is the primary form of exchange and the basis of the social system in primitive societies. It could also be said that a society is first and foremost an exchange system and that the gift is the primary form of exchange.

Lévi-Strauss would espouse this idea and would see exchange as the first fact of social life. A society is first of all an exchange network: in *Structural Anthropology*, Lévi-Strauss states that men exchange wealth or goods, words and women. Here once again we have Rousseau's social contract; and Lévi-Strauss goes on to see primitive societies as the purest, almost idealized expression of humankind. Yet this strain of romanticism, heavily laced with exoticism, would prevent him conceiving of anthropology as a science, in other words as a body of knowledge aimed at building models. Lévi-Strauss thus seems to mix the particularizing relativism* of the Anglo-American approach with the rationalist* universalizing tradition of the French. At times he asserts his faith in cultural diversity (e.g. in *Race and History*), at other times he looks for the symbolic origins of society; while underscoring differences, he is actually interested in similarities. In fact that is perhaps what is so attractive about his approach to anthropology: he depicts "the savage" as someone close to "us", someone who tells us something about ourselves, but at the same time he does not strip him completely of his strangeness. The savage is noble and intelligent, deserving of our admiration and attention, to be sure, but he is still a savage.

Boas and Diffusionism

The influences discussed above are well known and could almost be described as conventional. Nevertheless it seems to me that we must not neglect the time Lévi-Strauss spent in the United States and the intellectual climate he found there. During his stay, he associated with students of Boas, whose ideas on cultural determinism* he shared only in moderation. Despite a certain avowed Durkheimian influence, his anthropology is no doubt less of the social than of the cultural variety. His passion for the arts, for masks and for made objects found particularly fertile soil in America. And he himself said how much he admired the American Indian specialists of the Bureau of American Ethnology.

Lévi-Strauss' anthropology sometimes has an old-fashioned air about it. He was fond of old prints, catalogs, museums, old collections. By their frozen character, detached from the human context into which they were born, museum pieces are no doubt more amenable to structural analysis than are conflicts, beliefs, ambitions or passions. Here too Lévi-Strauss reveals a certain ambiguity: his taste for the concrete material object is a mere pretext for indulging in abstraction. The craftsman, the creator or the maker of these works does not really exist for him. If Lévi-Strauss likes the concrete, it is as a means to discover the abstract it conceals.

–2–

Beyond Empiricism

A World of the Mind

There is a form of Cartesianism, a liking for reason and logic, that underlies structural anthropology as a whole. It is the mind that fashions, organizes and structures the world. One wonders if this taste for abstraction, reason, intelligence may not stem from Lévi-Strauss' family background and his French culture. When it comes to religion, for example, his parents were non-believers and did not celebrate the Jewish holidays. Lévi-Strauss would inherit this relative indifference to religious phenomena, which he reduced to a few stereotyped expressions or at least to well-regulated institutionalized forms.

For Lévi-Strauss, anthropology is above all a way of thinking, a sort of empirical philosophy that does not aim at changing the world: "I am not saying it cannot serve. But it isn't what I ask of it, it is not the part of it that satisfies me."[4] Even Marxism, which he says influenced him, appears in his writings as no more than a theoretical system, a way of thinking about the world of knowledge. Despite his own claims and a few Althusserian attempts to bring his work into line with Marxism, his thought was and would remain fundamentally ahistorical and apolitical. What he claims to owe to Marxism seems of a purely intellectual nature – was it perhaps simply a concession to the times, a way of gaining recognition from his peers in the social sciences? After his return from the United States, he made political commitments only with reluctance and regularly refused to support militant causes. In this he was always a model of integrity and cannot be charged with demagogy.

Confronted with a mask, a myth, or more simply the native he has come upon, he sees a "problem" crying out to be solved. Human beings move him little: a living society disconcerts him, he admits in *Tristes Tropiques*. And in the same work, he clearly sets out the principles of the structuralist approach:

> The customs of a community, taken as a whole, always have a particular style and are reducible to systems. I am of the opinion that the number of such systems is not unlimited and that … human societies, like individuals, never create absolutely, but merely choose certain combinations from an ideal repertoire that it should be possible to define.[5]

At the beginning of *The Way of the Masks*, he observes: "This art posed a problem to me which I could not resolve."[6] The study of primitive life raises questions, and the anthropologist responds by trying to find solutions to these problems, or rather to retrace the intellectual process of the indigenous peoples whom Lévi-Strauss invites to share in his undertaking. For they too are entirely dedicated to resolving intolerable contradictions. That is why he asserts, in *Totemism*, that, in order to understand the facts associated with totemism, one must enter into mental communion, as it were, with the savage mind. The solution to such problems will not be found in empirical reality, but in ways of thinking.

The Illusion of Transparency

The real world, such as it offers itself up to observation, is a mere illusion, a delusion that must be transcended. We see here how Lévi-Strauss distances himself from Malinowski's principles of participant observation, according to which knowledge derives directly from experience in the field. Lévi-Strauss rejects such empiricism; the manifest world is only a veneer, the key to understanding is always in the latent material: it is hidden, and the anthropologist's task precisely is to seek it out.

Observable empirical categories are tools that can be used to pry out the abstract notions and link up propositions, he writes in *The Raw and the Cooked.*

In various passages, Lévi-Strauss explains that it is futile to ask natives their reasons for acting as they do or the meaning of their practices: unfailingly, they reply that they have no idea or that their ancestors have always lived this way, but they are incapable of giving a satisfactory explanation. In *Structural Anthropology*, for instance, he rejects the idea that empirical observation of any society reveals "universal motivations" and in his *Introduction to the Work of Marcel Mauss* he denies the importance of "indigenous conceptions", which one must get beyond if one is to reach an "underlying reality". As Dubuisson[7] rightly remarks, the real remains vague and disorderly for Lévi-Strauss, whose project is to bring some (intellectual) order to this jumble: beneath the apparent disorder, however, there are unchanging laws and rules.

What about the Unconscious?

Lévi-Strauss is thus led to define social anthropology as a science concerned with the "unconscious conditions of social life".[8] In keeping with such a definition, the analysis should penetrate the "unconscious structure" of each institution. In order to do this, the anthropologist must study the variations and transformations of an institution and discover behind these differences "one single pattern", the "structure underlying the multiple formulations".[9] We will examine what is meant by structure* in the next chapter. Here we will simply note that Lévi-Strauss' use of the notion of the unconscious* is not really clear. If he means "unconscious" in the psychoanalytical sense, his definition of social anthropology is unacceptable, as Leach has pointed out.[10] Moreover, it is not because people are unable to explain a custom that the key to the explanation lies buried in a purported unconscious. Furthermore, there is not always a rupture between the indigenous theory and that of the anthropologist. For instance, I was struck to hear the Paraiyar of South India talk about patrilateral cross-cousin marriage in terms of reciprocity: a woman who has been given must be returned, they explained to me, thus formulating the crux of Lévi-Strauss' explanation.

In *Tristes Tropiques*, Lévi-Strauss cites psychoanalysis as one of his three intellectual mainstays.[11] The fact that the other two are Marxism and geology adds to my perplexity, which is now verging on incredulity. While much has been written about the connection between structuralism and psychoanalysis, it is all essentially speculative. In the first place, Lévi-Strauss constantly confuses "what is not conscious" with the unconscious. Yet the nuance is important. There are many things of which we are not conscious, but which are not part of the unconscious, in the psychoanalytical sense (insofar as such a thing exists), namely things connected with earlier experiences that are supposed to guide our actions and which can only be brought to the conscious level by means of a therapy. Lévi-Strauss is no doubt occasionally tempted to go that far: for instance, in his *Introduction to the Work of Marcel Mauss*, he asserts that the unconscious "would thus be the mediating term between self and others".[12] If we follow him down this road, relations between people would be largely determined by elements beyond their control and that are forced on them.

Here we find one of the basic principles of structuralism, which can be described as a device for obliterating time and the individual. However, Lévi-Strauss did not take the notion of unconscious that far in either his methodology or his work. Generally speaking, it is more productive to consider that Lévi-Strauss uses "unconscious" to mean, above all, not conscious or simply not explicit.

At the epistemological level, however, this means that the psychoanalyst's role is a central one: explanations cannot be derived from the observation of reality, but must be the result of reducing reality to models.

–3–

Structuralism

The foregoing considerations contain many elements typical of structuralism. While Lévi-Strauss is one of the most famous representatives of this approach, it was not his invention. As I have stressed, structuralism is not really a method, it is something of a mixture, and one would be hard put to find a common thread linking all so-called structuralist studies. We will of course limit ourselves here to the work of Lévi-Strauss, which poses a problem. The British anthropologist Ernest Gellner admits that, after having read and translated Lévi-Strauss, he was incapable of saying what structuralism actually is.[13] Likewise, Raymond Boudon showed the highly imprecise nature, which he tactfully termed polysemy, of the concept of structure.[14] Lévi-Strauss himself has been relatively unforthcoming about the definition of structure, and one observer even remarked that Lévi-Strauss resigned himself to talk about it only in response to his critics.

Social Structure

British anthropology between the two wars progressively turned to the study of social structures, and for that reason it came to be known as "social anthropology". Without question, the most influential figure in this current was Radcliffe-Brown. Even if Lévi-Strauss sometimes happens to use the concept of "social structure"*, it is once more a manner of speaking, for it can be said that this notion does not actually belong to the conceptual arsenal of structuralism. It comes from structural-functionalism* and refers to those social relations that British anthropologists do not hesitate to regard as an empirical, almost observable, reality. The disagreement between Radcliffe-Brown and Lévi-Strauss on this point is particularly telling. According to Radcliffe-Brown, there is no break between social structure and empirical reality; and therefore the way to reconstruct the social structure of a society is by observing it. Here is what he writes to Lévi-Strauss:

> When I pick up a particular sea shell on the beach, I recognize it as having a particular structure, so that I can say there is a form of structure characteristic of the species.[15]

Structure is therefore what remains when the components change, it is the particular arrangement of the parts of a whole, and a social structure is an arrangement of persons in relation to each other. Radcliffe-Brown was thus to give a special impetus to the study of kinship by viewing it as a system.

Many have pointed to the discontinuity between the two conceptions of structure, but Lévi-Strauss made no mistake and acknowledged his debt to Radcliffe-Brown. Moreover, their theoretical rift did not rule out a relative similarity between the work of the two men, particularly in their approach to kinship. It is possible that Lévi-Strauss' study of the "atom of kinship", in *Structural Anthropology*, indeed owes much to Radcliffe-Brown's own analyses.[16]

In both cases, at the very least, interplay of relations prevails over components; an attempt is made to emphasize the connections between persons rather than the persons themselves: the relationship between mother's brother and sister's son does not depend on the personalities of the two men, it is a formal relation imposed on everyone, a social relation. Such an approach reduces reality to a set of general, formal characteristics that do not vary. Thus it can be said that in some societies this relation is positive (+), whereas in others it is negative (-). In other words, the complexity of the world and the ambiguity of all human relations are reduced to an invariable general feature.

Structure

Nevertheless, Lévi-Strauss was determined to go beyond this first stage, and he preferred the concept of "structure" to that of "social structure", even if he sometimes uses the two interchangeably. He holds that structure cannot be reduced to "objective reality"; it "concerns models patterned on this reality".[17] His position is thus opposed to that of Radcliffe-Brown, who sees structures everywhere: "Whenever we use the term structure, we are referring to some sort of ordered arrangement of parts or components. A musical composition has a structure, and so does a sentence. A building has a structure, so does a molecule or an animal", he writes in *Structure and Function in Primitive Society*.[18] It is from this perspective that one could talk about the "Nuer social structure". Yet it is precisely therein that the difference between the structural-functional tradition and structuralism proper lies. In the latter, and in Lévi-Strauss in particular, one should in principle not speak of the structure of a particular object.

It is easier to say what structure is not than what it actually is. In *The Uses of Structuralism*[19], Boudon writes that he is not sure whether the term structure has the same meaning in *The Raw and the Cooked* as in *The Elementary Structures of Kinship*. One can but confirm the ambiguity. Not only are the general considerations on structure many in number, but the variety of uses are just as numerous. Sometimes the notion of structure is associated with that of social structure, and at other times with that of model or system.

Nor does saying that structure is an abstract concept resolve all the problems, for the question then arises of whether or not this abstraction is localized: is it a formal, mathematical model or, on the contrary, a construction specific to the human mind? At times it seems that things (myths, kinship …) have a structure: sometimes, for instance, Lévi-Strauss states that the analysis must get down to the "unconscious structure" underlying each institution. At these times he is not very far from

Radcliffe-Brown. It is this perspective that tends to prevail in *The Elementary Structures*. At other times, structure seems to be a pure abstraction, a mathematical model and therefore an intellectual construction. Lévi-Strauss has always been tempted by a formalization, a mathematicalization of social life. In practice, however, he fails to convince.

It is in *Structural Anthropology* that he most clearly explains what is to be understood by the term structure.[20] To be sure, this definition does not eliminate all the problems, and it is not necessarily found in Lévi-Strauss' research. Nevertheless, since it is almost the only explicit attempt at a definition, it is not uninteresting to repeat the principal features here. To merit the name of structure, models must fulfill four conditions:

1. The structure exhibits the characteristics of a system: a change in any one of the elements results in changes in all the rest.
2. For any given model there should be a possibility of ordering a series of transformations resulting in a group of models of the same type.
3. Properties 1 and 2 make it possible to predict how the model will react to modification of one of its elements.
4. The model should be constructed so as to account for all of the observed facts.

Contrary to what the author claims, this is not so much a definition as a set of essential features. The ambiguity remains: the first condition can thus be paraphrased by saying that the structure is a model that forms a system. This first condition is rather badly phrased in fact, in the sense that structure is normally more a set of relations, that is a particular arrangement of relations between elements; it is therefore not the modification of one of its elements that produces the changes, but the modification of some relation between the elements. In *Structural Anthropology II,* Lévi-Strauss comes back to this idea, with the statement that one of the fundamental rules of structural analysis is that the analysis can never consider the terms alone, it must grasp the relations that connect them.[21]

–4–

The Primacy of the Mind

The Symbolic Origins of Society

Structuralism does not regard observable reality as its primary object of study. The social sphere in this case is considered to be merely a realization of the properties of the human mind. In other words, and contrary to Durkheim for whom, according to Piaget,[22] the social determines thought, Lévi-Strauss asserts the primacy of the intellect, of the mind, over the social. Just as speech is the realization of language, so the social derives its fundamental properties from the human mind. Or to put it another way, we can say with Leach that, in the structuralist perspective, cultures are the product of the human brain.[23] It is in this sense that Lévi-Strauss, in his *Introduction to the Work of Marcel Mauss*, affirms that Mauss wanted to constitute a sociological theory of symbolism, whereas in reality one must look for the "symbolic origins of society".[24]

One could thus speak of cognitive sociology; however, it is not altogether clear what is to be understood by "mind", and it is in this sense that I have used the terms "brain", "mind" and "intellect" interchangeably. Like language, the symbolic systems formed by cultures exist outside the individuals that inherit them; yet it is hard to see how they could exist without these individuals. Here the analogy with language assumes its full meaning: the social system is a "symbolic", conceptual (*idéel*) system conceived in and of the same order as the mind, and its existence precedes that of the individual. According to this reasoning, then, there is a set of rules that, like language, are used by people to create the world.

The social system is thus the realization of the capacities of the human mind. Or to put it another way, thinking processes are realized, actualized, made concrete. The social world is the realization of the categories of the brain. Lévi-Strauss usually looks at social phenomena from a general, theoretical standpoint and seems to be less interested in concrete societies. When it comes to myths, for example, he looks not so much for the relations between these and the societies that tell them as for the general foundations of "mythic thought". Here we touch on a crucial aspect of Lévi-Strauss' work: simplifying, it could be said that the questions at the root of his sociology are whether people tell myths the world over; why men marry their cross cousins; why they worship totems*? If such things are done everywhere, it is because people are endowed with the intellectual equipment that leads them to act in this way. While the answers to these questions are not always satisfying, the questions remain fundamental, and the very fact of having asked them while attempting to find answers is enough to show the salience of Lévi-Strauss' undertaking.

Binary Oppositions

According to the structuralists, dichotomous thinking is one way the human mind functions, and one of its fundamental properties. Thought finds a certain coherence in the constitution of systems of (most often binary) opposition. It is in this way that ideas are conceived in a coherent and even systematic fashion: edible vs. non-edible, low vs. high, raw vs. cooked, nature vs. culture and so on. In other words, since culture, like language, is a system of signs, the signs are placed in opposition and above all two by two. A sign exists only in relation to other signs, it has no reality on its own, outside the relation that opposes it to other signs. High exists only with respect to low.

The task of the analyst will therefore be to show how these oppositions form a system and acquire meaning. To take a famous example, the study of the myths recounting the origin of cooked food reveals that the opposition between raw and cooked is merely the expression of the more general opposition between nature and culture. Such reduction of a complex rite or myth to a series of oppositions became one of the key elements of structural analysis. To achieve their goal, structuralists would sometimes stray so far from reality that their analysis amounted to a veritable intellectual juggling act, which may have seemed appealing at the time, but which today leaves one somewhat dumbfounded.

The Rejection of History

There are many testimonials to the value of history in Lévi-Strauss' work. In fact, he continually affirms the importance of the historical approach. He even goes so far as to reproach Malinowski and Radcliffe-Brown for their rejection of history. And yet it would be hard to find the slightest trace of historical analysis in his writings. Structuralism is indeed a machine for obliterating time; the idea of structure itself is contrary or at least resistant to change.

By its reduction of the social to a symbolic system, structuralism conveys a certain philosophy of history or of becoming. What matters, when it comes to humans and their societies, are the formal rules that bind everyone and for all time. If society is a system, it is also an equilibrium; everything is done with a view to maintaining a balance and proper functioning. A system is not made for change. Furthermore men do not have much elbow room; the rules are forced on them without their being able to do anything about it.

Whereas some would make a structuralist of Marx, the philosopher Henri Lefebvre[25] was more astute and showed the gulf that separates Marxism from structuralism. Structuralism, he argues, contests the flow of history. In Marx, on the other hand, "immobility is death", what matters is becoming. Lévi-Strauss is concerned with that which is timeless, frozen. He prefers rites to beliefs, rules to trends, and more generally synchrony to diachrony. A structuralist theory of social change is unthinkable.

The debate that was to oppose Georges Balandier to Lévi-Strauss is rooted in this difference in ways of looking at the world and society. Balandier would favor social dynamics, and the role of anthropology, as he saw it, would be precisely to highlight the contemporary changes under way in primitive societies.[26]

The Culinary Triangle

Sometimes structural analysis set off in such directions that one could legitimately wonder if it were some kind of joke. For instance, in a text entitled "The Culinary Triangle", Lévi-Strauss gives free rein to some thoughts that are surprising to say the least:

"A tetrahedron will replace the recipe triangle, making it possible to raise a third axis, that of oil, in addition to those of air and water. The grilled will remain at the apex, but in the middle of the edge joining smoked and fried one can place roasted-in-the-oven (with the addition of fat), which is opposed to roasted-on-the-spit (without this addition). Similarly, on the edge running from fried to boiled will be braising (in a base of water and fat), opposed to steaming (without fat, and at a distance from the water). The plan can be still further developed, if necessary, by addition of the opposition between animal and vegetable foodstuffs (if they entail differentiating methods of cooking) and by the distinction of vegetable foods into cereals and legumes, since unlike the former (which one can simply grill), the latter cannot be cooked without water or fat, or both (unless one were to let the cereals ferment, which requires water but excludes fire during the process of transformation) … Thus, we can hope to discover … how the cooking of a society is a language in which it unconsciously translates its structure – or else resigns itself, still unconsciously, to revealing its contradictions."[27]

Notes

1. J.-J. Rousseau, *Essay on the Origin of Languages*, in Jean-Jacques Rousseau, *The Discourses and Other Early Political Writings*, edited by Victor Gourevitch, Cambridge, Cambridge University Press, 1997, pp. 247–99.
2. F. de Saussure, *Course in General Linguistics*, edited by Charles Bally and Albert Sechehaye with the collaboration of Albert Riedlinger, translated and annotated by Roy Harris, Lasalle, IL, Open Court, 1983.
3. M. Mauss, *The Gift: The Form and Reason for Exchange in Archaic Societies*, translated by W.D. Halls, foreword by Mary Douglas, New York, W.W. Norton, 1990.
4. C. Lévi-Strauss, *Conversations with Claude Lévi-Strauss*, with Didier Eribon, translated by Paula Wissing, Chicago, University of Chicago Press, 1991, p. 67.
5. C. Lévi-Strauss, *Tristes Tropiques*, translated by John and Doreen Weightman, New York, Penguin, 1992, p. 178.
6. C. Lévi-Strauss, *The Way of the Masks*, translated by Sylvia Modelski, Seattle, University of Washington Press, 1982, p. 10.
7. D. Dubuisson, *Mythologies du XXe siècle (Dumézil, Lévi-Strauss, Eliade),* Lille, Presses Universitaires de Lille, 1993, p. 137.
8. C. Lévi-Strauss, *Structural Anthropology*, translated by Claire Jaubson and Brooke Grundfest Schoepf, New York, Basic Books, 1963, p. 23.
9. C. Lévi-Strauss, *Anthropologie Structurale*, Paris, Plon, 1958, p. 29.
10. E. Leach, *Lévi-Strauss*, London, Fontana, 1970, p. 19.
11. *Lévi-Strauss, Tristes Tropiques* (English edition), p. 57.
12. C. Lévi-Strauss, *Introduction to the Work of Marcel Mauss*, translated by Felicity Baker, London, Routledge and Kegan Paul, 1987, p. 35.
13. E. Gellner, *Relativism and the Social Sciences*,

Cambridge, Cambridge University Press, 1985, p. 129.

14. R. Boudon, *The Uses of Structuralism*, translated by Michalina Vaughan and introduced by Donald MacRae, London, Heinemann, 1971.
15. Quoted by A. Kuper, *The Invention of Primitive Society: Transformations of an Illusion*, London, Routledge, 1988, p. 53.
16. Lévi-Strauss, *Structural Anthropology*, p. 72ff.
17. Ibid., p. 313.
18. A. R. Radcliffe-Brown, *Structure and Function in Primitive Society*, London, Cohen and West, 1952, p. 9.
19. R. Boudon, *A quoi sert la notion de "structure"? Essai sur la signification de la notion de structure dans les sciences humaines*, Paris, Gallimard, 1968, p. 18.
20. Lévi-Strauss, *Structural Anthropology*, pp. 279–80.
21. C. Lévi-Strauss, *Anthropologie structurale deux*, Paris, Plon, 1973, p. 107.
22. J. Piaget, *Structuralism*, translated by Chaninah Maschler, New York, Basic Books, 1970.
23. E. Leach, "Structuralism in Social Anthropology", in David Robey (ed.), *Structuralism: An Introduction*, Oxford, Clarendon Press, 1973, p. 38.
24. Lévi-Strauss, *Introduction to the Work of Marcel Mauss*, p. 21.
25. H. Lefebvre, *L'Idéologie structuraliste*, Paris, Le Seuil, 1971, p. 94.
26. For the debate with Balandier see F. Dosse, *Histoire du Structuralisme*, vol. one, *Le Champ du signe, 1945–1966*, Paris, La Découverte, 1991, pp. 324–33.
27. C. Lévi-Strauss, "The Culinary Triangle", in Carole Counihan and Penny Van Esterik (eds), *Food and Culture: A Reader*, New York, Routledge, 1997, pp. 28–35.

Part III
Tristes Tropiques

–1–

A Critique of Modernity

Lévi-Strauss' greatness today does not come from his formalism, which now seems so outdated. It lies rather in the ambiguities, the contradictions, the dead ends into which his intelligence led him, perhaps in spite of himself. In this sense, *Tristes Tropiques*, our focus for the next few pages, remains a fundamental work that reveals the contradictions, ambitions and qualities, and not least the literary talent, of its author. Contrary to what some believe or claim, *Tristes Tropiques* is not marginal to Lévi-Strauss' production: it is a book that, more than any other no doubt, reveals the many aspects of his thought and above all the way he sees the world and the discipline of anthropology.

A Remarkable Book

Tristes Tropiques is first and foremost a tale of travel. It can even be considered a genre classic. Here the anthropologist breaks with the positivist tradition of classical anthropology, which rejects reflexivity of any kind. Its pages are studded with "I's", and some of his colleagues criticized Lévi-Strauss for "unbuttoning himself"(*sic*) in this way.[1] The jury of the Goncourt literary prize held the opposite view, however, and in a press release expressed their regret that they were unable to award their prize to Lévi-Strauss because the rules stipulated that only works of fiction were eligible. These conflicting reactions show the full extent of the ambiguity of the book: too literary for some, it was too ethnographical for others.

It is no small paradox that someone who wanted to make social anthropology an objective, formal science, having eliminated the subject, became publicly known through such a personal literary work. Nor is it an accident if this formalization of social life or the kind of law set out in "The Culinary Triangle" seem eccentric today, while the work we are concerned with here will be read for a long time to come. It is not only because we are living in a narcissistic era; besides, whatever Lévi-Strauss reveals about himself is not really essential. If *Tristes Tropiques* remains important today, it is because it speaks to us of the world, of ourselves and others, but also of the past, the present and the future. Beyond the voyage, it invites us to think; it ranges from wonder to regret. While claiming to hate travel, the author invites us along by showing how one is led from marvel to repulsion.

The account does not simply invite us to travel and tell us that some things are beautiful while others are less so, it also tells us *why* some things are attractive and others repellant. Constantly switching between genres, the author keeps us off balance, and we do not always know where we stand in a work that prides itself on talking about philosophy and, for instance, giving an empirical demonstration of the validity of Montaigne's or Rousseau's hypotheses. This is of course what makes the book so interesting and rich.

Remarkably enough, *Tristes Tropiques* is almost the only place in all of Lévi-Strauss' work where one finds ethnographic data recorded by him. In the rest, he works on material harvested by others. This book, intended to be the least scientific, is also the only one that made an empirical contribution to the discipline.

The Goncourt jury were not mistaken. *Tristes Tropiques* is written in a dazzling style; it is a classical piece worthy of the nineteenth century, and, although I am hardly qualified to, I would say it is one of the most remarkable literary works of the second half of the twentieth century. It was an immediate success with the public, but also with the intelligentsia, who quickly grasped its importance and heralded it for what it was worth.

Figures as diverse as Michel Leiris, René Etiemble, Jean Lacroix, Claude Roi, Georges Bataille or Raymond Aron declared their enthusiasm, while François-Régis Bastide spoke of another Chateaubriand. Except for Leiris, and for good reason, anthropologists reacted more critically. The most open-minded regarded the book as a parenthesis, a pleasant exercise, a "rather pointless pause in the long march toward intellective purity", in the ironic words of Clifford Geertz, who was no doubt the first specialist to take the work seriously.[2] The book had been written after several unsuccessful attempts to win a chair at the Collège de France, and Lévi-Strauss thought the doors of that venerable institution would be closed to him forever, so great was the opposition of some to this kind of exercise. Nevertheless, as Dosse[3] points out in his *Histoire du structuralisme*, *Tristes Tropiques* enchanted numerous young researchers and drew them inevitably to social anthropology.

Indeed it can be said that no one was more successful than Lévi-Strauss in combining the lure of the exotic with intellectual rigor.

"Filth thrown into the face of mankind"

In Part I, we saw an intellectual of his time, more at ease no doubt in New York and Paris than among remote peoples. In fact he was not well acquainted with the latter, he had glimpsed them only from afar and somewhat furtively at that. It is perhaps for this reason that he paints them in a rather romantic light, as we will see in the following pages. Alternatively, Western society, in which he lives and the foundations of which he does not seem to have contested, appears to him as harmful when it encroaches on young nations.

It is very definitely Lévi-Strauss the romantic who regrets the development of third-world countries. In other words, our civilization is no good for poor countries. The romantic image of savages can only lead him to deplore their disappearance, to lament over the ruins of primitive cultures: "the whole of Asia is beginning to look like a dingy suburb", "shanty towns are spreading across Africa", "the first thing we see as we travel round the world is our own filth, thrown into the face of mankind."[4]

That is why travel is disappointing. One sets out in search of a world that no longer exists; the modern traveler "chas[es] after the vestiges of a vanished reality".[5] Rio de Janeiro repels him. São Paolo impresses him with its ugliness. The "major upheavals of history" lead to chaos. In Calcutta, surrounded by beggars and bitter commercial exploitation, all one can ultimately admire is a population seeking a cure for its ills:

> Filth, chaos, promiscuity, congestion; ruins, huts, mud, dirt; dung, urine, pus, humours, secretions and running sores: all the things against which we expect urban life to give us organized protection, all the things we hate and guard against at such great cost, all these by-products of cohabitation do not set any limitations on it in India. They are more like a natural environment which the Indian town needs to prosper.[6]

Here the "European" is at a loss; daily life is a constant repudiation of the concept of human relations. Lévi-Strauss confesses his confusion at the absence of all familiar landmarks in the presence of Indian reality. It is no longer humankind as he conceives it that he encounters here, but a foul, filthy mass that does nothing to elevate his mind. It is not here that he will find his charming savage, living outside of time and on whom, or at least on the image of whom, he was to found his sociological theories. This savage is, in the end, the product of a dream and not of this reality constituted by big cities. History is fundamentally frightening. Social anthropology thus appears as a refuge, the haven of a humanity on the brink of extinction.

> What frightens me in Asia is the vision of our own future which it is already experiencing. In the America of the Indians, I cherish the reflection, however fleeting it may now have become, of an era when the human species was in proportion to the world it occupied, and when there was still a valid relationship between the enjoyment of freedom and the symbols denoting it.[7]

With this critique of modern times, Lévi-Strauss inaugurates his praise of primitive life, or at any rate of a certain notion of primitive life, for the savage of which he is speaking is of his own making, fashioned out of his desire for a world in which exoticism is mingled with intelligence and goodness.

Against Progress

This is the only book in which Lévi-Strauss allows himself to criticize his own society and especially the idea of progress.

> I wish I had lived in the days of real journeys, when it was still possible to see the full splendour of a spectacle that had not yet been blighted, polluted and spoilt …[8]

Contact corrupts. The societies of Asia and South America are spoiled by modernity and are repugnant to it. Only groups living far from modern civilization have managed to retain their purity. Here Lévi-Strauss yields to the failing of those anthropologists who, as Leiris put it, have a

> wish to see the cultures on which they have expended their efforts undergo the minimum change … so as to be able to go on studying them or to delight in the spectacle they offer.[9]

Leiris goes on to castigate those he regards as worshipers of progress who, because of their failure to take notice, may fail to appreciate the immense treasure accumulated by humankind on either side of the narrow furrow on which their own gaze is riveted.

For Lévi-Strauss there is no better example of humankind than the one he encountered in the Amazonian forest. Among the Nambikwara and the Tupi-Kawahib, he discovered the brotherhood of Man, which contrasts with the overpopulated Indian subcontinent where everything is dehumanized.

With Lévi-Strauss, the savage becomes fashionable. But his criticism of progress is not directed at the West. What he regrets is that primitive societies are driven out of existence. He does not question the idea of progress of his own culture as such, or lifestyle, rather he objects to the way it is applied to other parts of the world. The distinction he makes in *Structural Anthropology II* between "cold societies" and "hot societies" is typical of this separation of the world into "them" and "us".[10] The first are characterized by lack of change, by being "close to zero on the historical temperature scale", and because of this they are purveyors of dreams. Progress is at best a relative concept, and it is not cumulative.

Lévi-Strauss' depiction of the savage is striking in its eighteenth-century naivety. It is also reminiscent of the longing for the countryside, the exaltation of rusticity that we find in George Sand; the peasant of the Berry region has become a Bororo hunter, but we are all the more drawn to him because we see him through the filter of our own desires.

Is not the criticism of progress one more way for the anthropologist to fulfill personal fantasies and to deny other cultures what is the norm in his or her own: health, modernity and material well-being? The anthropologist is thus turned into what the French would call a *conservateur*, playing on the double meaning of "conservative" in one's values and "conservator" of a museum. Lévi-Strauss would like to preserve tradition, to make the world into a museum, but at the same time to call a halt to all forms of "progress", a notion that is no longer part of his vocabulary so strongly is perfection associated with purity, tradition and stagnation. This is all the more remarkable as such anthropologists have not translated their preoccupations into political or practical terms.

–2–

Charming Savages

Civilization does not seem to be made for the inhabitants of the tropics, whom Lévi-Strauss has clothed in the robes of tradition. Compared to the monsters and monstrosities of the city, the savage is good and worthy of note. This apology of primitive life is not neutral. Once again, it is not the savage lifestyle that Lévi-Strauss finds attractive, but an image of his own making. What one finds in his remote villages is not the horror of a struggle for survival but a basically intelligent being skilled in abstraction and speculation, capable of producing highly stylized works of art worthy of the most illustrious artists.[11]

A Disappointing Encounter

Tristes Tropiques, as I have stressed, is the only one of Lévi-Strauss' books that contains actual ethnographic material. The data is meager and somewhat lost amid all the philosophical, demographic and historical considerations; furthermore it is laced with the author's impressions; he no more than grazes the surface of the indigenous culture. In order for those studied to remain good and pure, Lévi-Strauss must maintain the distance or risk seeing them lose their noble naivety. Moreover, and contrary to the cardinal rule of classical ethnology, for which the encounter is the source of knowledge, Lévi-Strauss considers that the true source of knowledge lies elsewhere:

> I had wanted to reach the extreme limits of the savage; it might be thought that my wish had been granted, now that I found myself

> among these charming Indians whom no other white man had ever seen before and who might never be seen again. After an enchanting trip up-river, I had certainly found my savages. Alas! they were only too savage. Since their existence had only been revealed to me at the last moment, I was unable to devote to them the time that would have been essential to get to know them. The limited resources at my disposal, the state of physical exhaustion in which my companions and I now found ourselves … allowed me no more than a short busman's holiday instead of months of study. There they were, all ready to teach me their customs and beliefs, and I did not know their language. They were as close to me as a reflection in a mirror; I could touch them, but I could not understand them. I had been given at one and the same time, my reward and my punishment. Was it not my mistake, and the mistake of my profession, to believe that men are not always men? that some are more deserving of interest and attention because they astonish us by the colour of their skin and their customs? I had only to succeed in guessing what they were like for them to be deprived of their strangeness: in which case, I might just as well have stayed in my village.[12]

The notion of a seamless continuum between experience and reality is a bias: experience does not enable us to understand reality. Quite the contrary. If we are to grasp reality for what it is, we must repudiate experience and remove ourselves to an objective world that has no room for sentimentalism. If we want to get to know "savage" peoples, we discover that it is no use approaching them physically, for it is not by "touching them" that we can come to "understand" them; what we must do, on the contrary, is reduce the expressions of their culture to abstract models of relations.

The Savage to the Aid of Rousseau

Reading *Tristes Tropiques*, one sometimes gets the impression that it is as much about Montaigne and Rousseau as it is about indigenous peoples. When Lévi-Strauss speaks of them, he betrays his lack of knowledge by reflections that seem "impressionistic" to say the least: he "senses" their "immense kindness";[13] polygamous marriage does not give rise to any kind of bitterness on the part of the wives;[14] "mother and child together provide a gay and charming picture";[15] the natives are "almost always merry and gay".[16] This idyllic picture is more the result of hasty impressions than of attentive observation of reality. Lévi-Strauss' fieldwork seems to have been limited to wanderings in the Amazonian forest interspersed with brief encounters that merely confirmed old literary clichés about "the good savage".

Yet the task that Lévi-Strauss set for himself is no less vast or noble for that: he wanted "to show the considerable support given … by contemporary anthropology to the theories put forward by eighteenth-century thinkers".[17] Rousseau demonstrated a profound intuition about society and had no need to see savages in order to understand them and hence to reveal the foundations of society: namely that the contract and consent constitute the "raw materials of social life". Giving and giving in return are thus almost natural values; exchange does not have to be constructed, it is automatic. Even the chief's political power is subject to the constraints of reciprocity. Here "strife is replaced by barter".[18]

Solving Problems

The ethnographic analyses set out in *Tristes Tropiques* always follow the same pattern and, far from being specific to this work, they are typical of Lévi-Strauss' method in general. He begins by presenting the object to be studied, often a frozen expression of the culture, a mask, a myth, a rite. This element becomes a twofold problem: on the one hand, it is the expression of a problem that the people under study were obliged to solve and, on the other, it is a problem for the analyst, who must discover the meaning it holds. The anthropologist will therefore retrace the intellectual path taken by the "savage" mind, which shows, if it were still necessary, the high degree of intellectual sophistication involved. If the solution appears simple, and even naive, it is only an appearance, for the meaning is hidden. The object of study is the expression of the quasi-philosophical solution to a contradiction. In other words, nothing is left to chance in social life; a people's customs taken as a whole "form a system".[19] Tattooed designs, for instance, follow a set of motifs and styles corresponding to a theory that must be discovered.[20] Simplicity is always deceptive: indigenous art calls for most careful examination; it obeys requirements of symmetry and asymmetry by adopting a symmetrical composition executed along an oblique axis.

When all is said and done, Caduveo or Bororo art is a means of resolving vexing philosophical and sociological contradictions: it expresses "the phantasm of a society ardently and insatiably seeking a means of expressing symbolically the institutions it might have, if its interests and superstitions did not stand in the way".[21] Instead of confronting their social contradictions, the indigenous peoples took to dreaming "in a transposed, and seemingly innocuous form: in their art".[22]

A Better World

"Primitive peoples manufacture little order through their culture. Today we call them underdeveloped peoples. But they manufacture very little entropy in their society. Roughly speaking, these societies are egalitarian, mechanical in nature, governed by the rule of unanimity ... Alternatively, civilized peoples manufacture a great deal of order in their culture, as is shown by mechanization and the great works of civilization, but they also manufacture a great deal of entropy in their society: social conflicts, political struggles, all those things against which we have seen primitive peoples take precautions, perhaps more consciously and systematically than we might have supposed."[23]

Notes

1. C. Lévi-Strauss, *De près et de loin: entretiens avec Didier Eribon*, Paris, Odile Jacob, 1988, p. 89.
2. C. Geertz, *Works and Lives: The Anthropologist as Author*, Cambridge, Polity Press, 1988, p. 33.
3. F. Dosse, *Histoire du structuralisme*, Paris, La Découverte, 1991, 2 vols, p. 174.
4. C. Lévi-Strauss, *Tristes Tropiques*, translated by John and Doreen Weightman, New York, Penguin Books, 1992, p. 38.
5. Ibid., p. 43.
6. Ibid., p. 134.
7. Ibid., p. 150.
8. Ibid., p. 43.
9. M. Leiris, *Cinq études d'ethnologie*, Paris, Gonthier, 1969, pp. 90–1.
10. C. Lévi-Strauss, *Anthropologie structurale deux*, Paris, Plon, 1973, p. 40.
11. C. Lévi-Strauss, *Race et histoire*, Paris, Unesco, 1952, p. 31.
12. Lévi-Strauss, *Tristes Tropiques* (English edition), p. 332–3.
13. Ibid., p. 293.
14. Ibid., 313
15. Ibid., p. 283.
16. Ibid., p. 281.
17. Ibid., p. 314.
18. Ibid., p. 303.
19. Ibid., p. 178.
20. Ibid., p. 187.
21. Ibid., p. 197.
22. Ibid., p. 196.
23. G. Charbormier (ed.), *Entretiens avec Claude Lévi-Strauss*, Paris, Plon/Julliard, 1961, p. 47; translated for this book by Nora Scott.

Part IV
Kinship

–1–

The Incest Taboo

All of the great anthropologists have distinguished themselves in the study of kinship. Lévi-Strauss is no exception, and in 1949 he published the original French edition of *The Elementary Structures of Kinship*, which, once again, is a major work and a great classic of sociological literature. It is not by chance that this work is dedicated to Lewis Morgan, and that its title is a paraphrase of a book by Durkheim. What might appear presumptuous actually is not: this study belongs to the family of great works. Kinship would continue to interest Lévi-Strauss, but the announced volume on complex structures never appeared. As I have already stressed, Lévi-Strauss has always been able to draw a fairly large audience to domains that are both technical and sophisticated. This is particularly true in this case, for here is a dense, difficult and long book dealing with a very specific type of marriage, namely unions between cross cousins, a practice not found in industrialized societies. Yet the book was well received and was widely discussed by a broad range of personalities, Simone de Beauvoir, for instance. And this is because, as was often the case, Lévi-Strauss demonstrated his ability to reduce individual practices to the general problems of living in society.

The Basics

Nature and Culture

The human is at once a biological and a social being whose behavior is at times guided by his or her nature, at times by culture, but it is not always easy to tell which is which. Where does nature stop and culture begin? These questions have never ceased to preoccupy anthropologists.

According to Lévi-Strauss, culture begins with the rule. Wherever there are rules, we can be sure we are dealing with culture, for the rule is specific; it institutes an order. By the same token, nature deals in universals. Whatever is constant necessarily falls outside the domain of the institutions, customs and techniques by which groups distinguish themselves and oppose others:

> Let us suppose then that everything universal in man relates to the natural order, and is characterized by spontaneity, and that everything subject to a norm is cultural and is both relative and singular.[1]

There is one institution, however, that belongs to both domains at once, and that is the incest prohibition. In effect, it constitutes a rule, but a rule that, alone among all the rules of society, possesses at the same time a universal character. For marriage is never permitted between all categories of close kin. In short, the incest prohibition possesses at once the universal character of tendencies and drives, and the coercive character of laws and institutions. It could therefore be said that the incest taboo marks the passage from nature to culture; it expresses at the same time our animal nature and our human nature.

Such is at least the view of Lévi-Strauss, for things may not be that simple. It does not seem to me either that the incest prohibition is all that specific or that it is the object of a "rule". Often there is no rule forbidding incest. In Western societies, for example, sexual relations between consenting adults are not forbidden. Many groups do not take the trouble to forbid these incestuous unions, so unnatural do they seem. Furthermore, when the rule actually exists, it specifies with whom it is forbidden to have sex, or rather whom one may not marry. In other words, the specificity of the prohibition in this passage from nature to culture does not seem to me to have been demonstrated. If we pursue the line of reasoning, we could say that eating also falls into both domains because eating is an eminently universal act that is also the object of cultural rules and taboos.

The Hidden Side Of Exchange

But that is not an essential point of the theory that interests us here. It is more important to note that the incest prohibition can be understood as a means to keep the nuclear family from closing in upon itself. Without the taboo on incest, the mother, the father and their children as a social unit could suffice unto themselves, which would be contrary to the rule of exchange that founds the social bond. In other words, the prohibition on marrying his mother or sister means that the man is forced to marry out of the basic family unit and therefore to contract "alliances" with "outsiders". As a cultural rule, the incest prohibition aims to ensure the group's survival, and the matrimonial institution – like economic life – is part of a system based on reciprocity. There can be no social life without reciprocity.

The incest taboo can thus be seen as the negative side of the exogamy* that forces every man to marry out of his own group.

The Circulation of Women

We have just seen that Lévi-Strauss regards exchange as the very basis of life in society. It is a fact on which society is founded. In other words, a social group is first of all an exchange system. Men, he goes on to say, exchange words, in their speech; they exchange wealth, goods, in their transactions; but they also exchange women.[2] Kinship is thus understood as a "system", that is as a network of relations that link men together. And it is the circulation of women that ensures the coherence of this system. In this way, kinship is a system of communication, a language and, of all social phenomena, it is one of the most amenable to "scientific analysis" because it can be made objective. Lévi-Strauss is tempted by a formal analysis of kinship relations. He would even encourage certain disciples to undertake a formal and even mathematical analysis of matrimonial exchange. However, he himself was to remain more modest in his analyses.

The Atom of Kinship

Let us momentarily leave aside *The Elementary Structures* and illustrate these principles using an analysis set out in *Structural Anthropology*.[3] Returning to Radcliffe-Brown's study of the avuncular relation* and carrying it further, Lévi-Strauss gives a rare example of what he means by "structure".

Radcliffe-Brown's Analysis

According to the British anthropologist Radcliffe-Brown,[4] the relations entertained between a boy and his mother's brother depend on the descent* system of his group. Owing to the structural principle of the equivalence of brothers and sisters, the father's sister is a kind of maternal father, whereas the mother's brother is a kind of paternal mother. This being the case, in matrilineal societies, which transmit the status of the mother's brother to his sister's son, relations between maternal uncle and sister's son are characterized by distance, respect and authority, whereas, conversely, the relationship between nephew and father's sister is tender, affectionate and close. Alternatively, in patrilineal societies, the relationship with the mother's brother is one of closeness, while that with the father's sister is simply an extension of the relationship with the father and is characterized by distance.

Lévi-Strauss' Critique

This study is considered to be one of the first structural analyses by Lévi-Strauss, who nevertheless underscores its limitations from the outset. Moreover, it is contradicted by the facts, for one finds matrilineal societies in which relations with the mother's brother are marked by closeness and, conversely, relations with the father's sister are not always distant in patrilineal societies.

Radcliffe-Brown's error was not to have understood that a structural analysis must take into account all of the family relations that go into a structure. To be complete and reliable, an analysis must include a far broader set of relations, namely: father/son, husband/wife, brother/sister, mother's brother/sister's son. Each relationship in this case must be analyzed with respect to the other three.

Why does the mother's brother come into this minimal family structure? Precisely because of the incest taboo that prevents the nuclear family closing in upon itself: the obligation to marry out of the nuclear family necessitates a second family, represented by the maternal uncle, the wife-giver par excellence. In other words, the smallest possible family structure, the "atom of kinship" necessarily includes the maternal uncle.

A Kinship Structure

Lévi-Strauss' analysis is a model of his method. He believes that the comparative method is a dead end because it requires the never-ending accumulation of examples. He likewise rejects all inductive methods. For a method to be truly scientific, it must select a limited number of cases that, as in scientific experiments, allow the construction of models.

In the case of kinship, the analyst has only to select four societies that enable him or her to elaborate a structure having universal validity. We recall that each relationship within the family is a function of the other three; in other words the avuncular relationship (mother's brother/sister's son = 4) stems from relations of alliance (husband/wife = 1), descent (father/son = 3) and consanguinity (brother/sister = 2). Since a structure is an equilibrium, these different relations will necessarily have to include two positive and two negative relations.

If one assigns a plus (+) or a minus (–) sign to each of these relations, every society must of necessity present a balanced table of plus and minus signs. Four examples of societies will be enough to illustrate a few of the cases that fit the table below.[5]

	1	*2*	*3*	*4*
Tonga	+	–	–	+
Lake Kutubu	–	+	+	–
Trobriand	+	–	+	–
Cherkess	–	+	–	+

The atom of kinship as a structure.

The avuncular relation, like any other relationship within the family, must be treated within a structure. In other words the mother's brother/sister's son relation (4) is to the brother/sister relation (2) as the father/son relation (3) is to the husband/wife relation (1).

Lévi-Strauss' analysis is tempting. Nevertheless one may wonder whether its validity does not lie in the largely arbitrary reduction of a complex family relation to a plus or minus sign. It would be difficult, for example, to apply such a procedure to American society. Of course, in traditional societies relations are perhaps more institutionalized, but they are never free of ambivalence.

–2–

Preferential Marriage

It is the actual object of *The Elementary Structures of Kinship* that now demands our attention, and more particularly marriage between first-degree cousins, which can be called "preferential marriage"*.

The Principle

Cross and Parallel Cousins

While all societies have a "negative marriage rule", that is to say prohibitions on marrying certain categories of kin, there are some, fewer, that have a positive rule, that is to say which "prescribe" a specific partner. In most cases this partner is a first-degree cousin, and more specifically a cross cousin. Cross cousins are children of "opposite-sex siblings" (the children of a brother *and* a sister). Conversely, parallel cousins are children of "same-sex siblings" (of two brothers *or* two sisters). For a variety of reasons, few societies prescribe marriage between parallel cousins, which is found for the most part in the Arab world and which encourages a certain closure of the family. Alternatively, encouragement for cross cousins to marry is found in numerous societies throughout the world.

Why Marry a Cousin?

Why is such a practice so widespread? Lévi-Strauss' work is of course an attempt to answer this question. It is for the most part an analysis of a mass of data, which he synthesizes.

If so many societies have this kind of "marriage rule", Lévi-Strauss says in *The Elementary Structures of Kinship*, it is because it enables them to express the exchange rule at the kinship level. In other words, through preferential marriage, these societies organize the exchange of women between groups and ensure that the gift of a woman is inevitably reciprocated. Secondly, this kind of marriage rests on the repetition of earlier marriages down through the generations, and thus enables the society to establish an alliance between the different exchanging units. That is why Lévi-Strauss' theory would come to be known as "alliance theory".

The Demonstration

Kinds of Exchanges and Cousins

The practice of exchange can be divided into *generalized* exchange and *restricted* exchange. Generalized exchange is found in those marriage systems in which exchange is direct and immediate. Restricted exchange, on the other hand, is characteristic of systems in which exchange is neither apparent nor direct. A boy can have three kinds of cross cousin: the matrilateral cross cousin, that is the mother's brother's daughter (MBD); the patrilateral cross cousin, that is the father's sister's daughter (FZD); and finally the bilateral cousin, namely one who is related on both the father's and the mother's side, in which case: MBD equals FZD.

Certain societies allow marriage with one type of cousin but not the other. In effect, the consequences of these marriages are very different sociologically, and we need to examine each in turn.

Marriage with the Bilateral Cousin

Bilateral cross-cousin marriage is more frequent in "dual organizations", "exogamous moiety systems", which are fairly rare but are found among the Aboriginal groups of Australia. In such systems the society is divided into two, sometimes totemic, groups that are exogamous, in other words one must choose one's spouse from the other "moiety". In these societies, marriage is almost naturally preferential because it joins two cross cousins. Furthermore, these cousins are related on both the mother's and the father's side, making them bilateral cousins. It is as though brothers were exchanging their sisters, and were doing so from one generation to the next. The name of the game is exchange: the gift of a girl is immediately reciprocated; each side is at the same time wife-giver and wife-taker with respect to the other side.

The diagram of this kind of marriage clearly shows the occurrence of exchange.

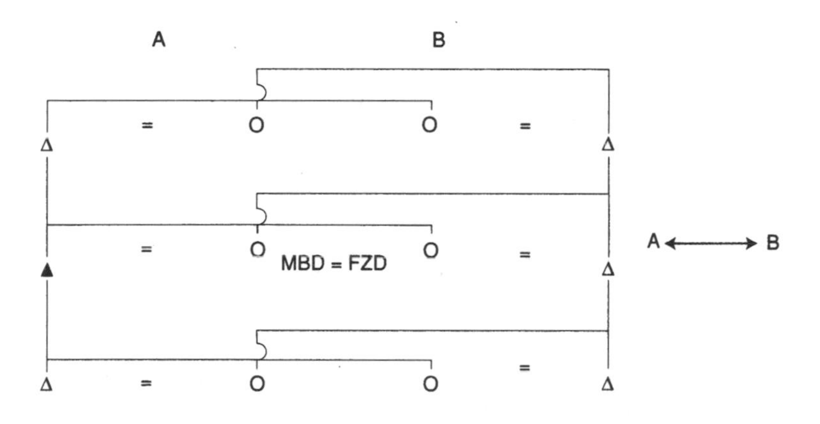

Theoretical model of bilateral cross-cousin marriage. O designates a woman, Δ a man; = stands for marriage; a horizontal line, the brother/sister link; a vertical line, the parent/child relationship.

The theoretical model shows the immediate reciprocity between moieties A and B. Furthermore each marriage in the diagram joins a man with his bilateral cross cousin. In Australia we also find societies divided into four or eight sections. In this case we are dealing with far more complicated situations, but Lévi-Strauss shows that exchange is always the prevailing principle.

Marriage with the Matrilateral Cross Cousin

In the case of restricted exchange, reciprocity is far less evident. This is particularly true of societies that prescribe marriage with the matrilateral cross cousin. In this case, we are dealing with a situation in which, although A gives women to B, it will never receive women from this group. A given group is thus either a wife-giver or a wife-taker with respect to another group, but never both at once. The theoretical model clearly shows this unilaterality.

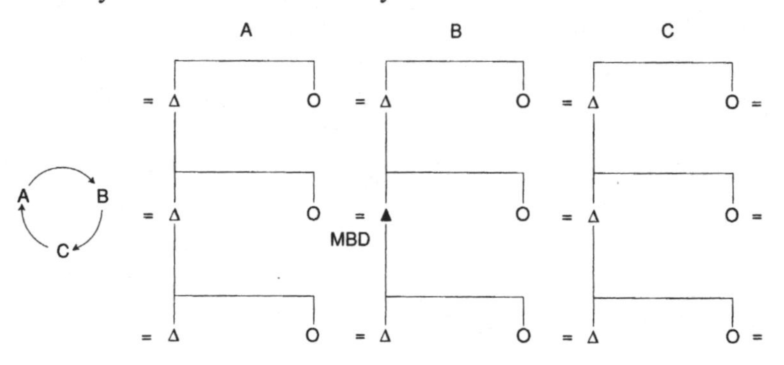

Theoretical model of matrilateral cross-cousin marriage.

However, A gives to B only because it is certain to receive women from a third group. The circularity is ensured by the system, which guaranties that the gift of a woman will be reciprocated. This reciprocity is by no means immediate, however. It presupposes an overall organization of society.

Such a solution harbors the seeds of status differentiation. The relationship that links two groups is, effectively, unilateral and because of this tends to introduce a certain difference between the two. Such a system can therefore have what Lévi-Strauss calls "aristocratic consequences" and lead to marriages between partners of unequal social status.[6] Moreover such a marriage rule presupposes a global arrangement of the society. Nevertheless, Lévi-Strauss emphasizes, exchange is still present, even if its functioning needs to be considered from a global standpoint to be visible.

Marriage with the Patrilateral Cross Cousin

Exchange is once again more apparent in the last type of marriage we will examine, namely patrilateral cross-cousin marriage, or marriage with the father's sister's daughter. This type of marriage gives rise to an altogether different situation from the standpoint of both matrimony and sociology.

The theoretical model clearly shows the fact that the gift of a girl to someone is automatically reciprocated, but in the following generation. The exchange is thus deferred by a generation: if I give my sister to a man, I will in turn receive my sister's daughter to give to my son.

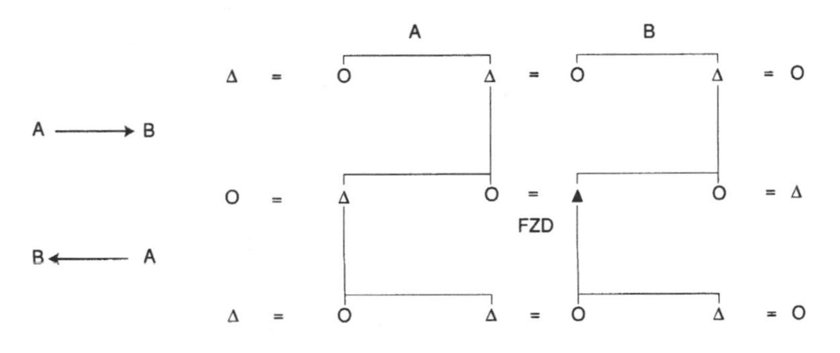

Theoretical model of patrilateral cross-cousin marriage.

Unlike marriage with the matrilateral cross cousin, patrilateral cross-cousin marriage does not demand an elaborate social structure. On the contrary, the families in this case are joined two by two and exchange women with each other. There are no matrimonial classes associated with such a form, and Rodney Needham was to say that one cannot speak of systems in this case.[7]

The obvious general conclusion, however, is that preferential marriage, by reproducing past marriages, seals the alliance and enables the groups to exchange women.

Discussion

The last few pages have presented only the broad lines of Lévi-Strauss' theory: its richness is far from being exhausted. Lévi-Strauss examines in particular the cases of India and China, provides an erudite discussion of Australia's sophisticated systems and, as always, brings out the fundamental issues involved in his research by his willingness to draw bold parallels and comparisons.

Towards a Formalization?

We have seen the enthusiasm and admiration aroused by *The Elementary Structures of Kinship*. It is, to my mind, Lévi-Strauss' most accomplished and remarkable book. Despite its technical character, the work avoids the pitfalls into which certain emulators have fallen by attempting to reduce the analysis of kinship to mathematical formulas. No doubt Lévi-Strauss encouraged these excesses by inciting his disciples to set out on this road, which he himself seems to have carefully avoided. Thus a few attempts at the mathematical formulation or modeling of marriage rules have made their appearance, but they have not amounted to much and certainly not to a more scientific approach.

Alternatively, it is somewhat astonishing to see that Lévi-Strauss spent almost no time on the terminology of kinship*. Yet kinship terms no doubt lend themselves more readily to a certain formalization; and it can even be said that they constitute a language.

Prescriptive or Preferential?

Lévi-Strauss' studies caused quite a stir in Great Britain, where supporters and opponents joined in pitched battle; Rodney Needham was one of the first to his defense. He translated several of his books into English and penned a short essay, entitled *Structure and Sentiment*, defending *The Elementary Structures* against criticism from the United States.

In this book, Needham notes that Lévi-Strauss uses the adjectives "prescriptive" and "preferential" interchangeably when speaking of cross-cousin marriage. And yet, Needham comments, the two terms do not have the same meaning, and Lévi-Strauss' book deals only with those cases in which marriage with the cousin is truly an obligation. The proper term is therefore "prescriptive".[8] In his reply, Lévi-Strauss argues that there is no real confusion and that it all depends on what level one is addressing: in theory, marriage is prescriptive, but in practice it is impossible to apply the rule in every case, and so it becomes preferential. Models, he goes on, are constructed after reality, but they do not reflect the full complexity of reality.[9]

Needham could not accept the clarification, which was in point of fact courteous, and thereafter devoted a good part of his time and his intellectual activity to criticizing the French anthropologist. It must be said that Needham was known for this sort of obsessive criticism, since he had formerly concentrated his energies on denigrating everything Radcliffe-Brown had written. He was to edit a collective volume on kinship studies that was quite pedantic,[10] with the contributing authors constantly pointing out the inanity of all concepts. Incapable of raising the level of the debate, Needham insinuates that Lévi-Strauss' sole merit is to have popularized in French the ideas previously published by Dutch anthropologists, a claim verging on libel. In addition, he contents himself with repeating that *The Elementary Structures* is an obscure work and that he no longer sees its significance. We have little trouble concurring with this last point.

Rules and Strategies

The critique by the sociologist Pierre Bourdieu is another matter altogether.[11] In *The Logic of Practice*, he adds an important dimension to *The Elementary Structures*: it is the notion of "rule". Bourdieu observes that, in those societies that have a "rule" dictating that a boy must marry his cousin, a relatively small proportion of marriages actually follow it. This observation, he says, leads us to revise the structuralist presuppositions and in particular to bring "social" agents into the sociological analysis. Social agents are not clockwork automatons that run according to formal rules imposed on them in the manner of mechanical laws.

Rules in no way obviate "strategies", in other words processes of invention and of deliberate action on the part of agents capable of manipulating the rules of society, of adapting and even of getting around them. The head of the family always has the freedom to play with the rules.

The Case of the Paraiyars

The case of the Paraiyars of South India, among whom I carried out fieldwork, is a good illustration of the import of Bourdieu's observations.[12] It is not uninteresting to note, first of all, that the Paraiyars, who encourage marriage with the patrilateral cross cousin, offer an explanation that seems to come straight out of *The Elementary Structures of Kinship*: "If I give my sister in marriage to a man", one Paraiyar comments, "I am minus a woman, and I must get another one: my sister will therefore have to give me her daughter so that she can marry my son." But at the same time, there is no formal obligation, and each father has a chance to get around the rule. Moreover, alliance comes before exchange in the strict sense, and, if need be, a man does not hesitate to give a second daughter. Finally, every marriage gives rise to discussions, equivocation and hesitation. People only give in after having gauged all the advantages and disadvantages. Even a marriage contracted according to the spirit of the rule is the outcome of strategies, for such a marriage presents clear advantages.

The Woman as Commodity

One does not necessarily have to be a militant feminist to voice reservations about the idea that women "circulate" between groups. Women are not a commodity, reduced to being mere objects passed from group to group. In places where residence after marriage is uxorilocal*, women do not circulate at all. Marriages are not always arranged by men either, and women often take an active part in the negotiations. This is very certainly the case among the Paraiyar. A girl's father cares what happens to her, and regards his son-in-law instead as the object to be carefully assessed. Likewise, women keep ties, rights and sometimes property in their natal group. No doubt the idea of "circulation" and "exchange" of women was intended by the author of *The Elementary Structures* to underscore the idea of kinship as a language. But this is a point of secondary importance, and the criticism in no way undermines the solidity of the work as a whole.

The Circulation of Women

"The emergence of symbolic thought must have required that women, like words, should be things that were exchanged ... But women could never become just a sign and nothing more, since even in a man's world she is still a person, and since in so far as she is defined as a sign she must be recognized as a generator of signs. In the matrimonial dialogue of men, woman is never purely what is spoken about; for if women in general represent a certain category of signs, destined to a certain kind of communication, each woman preserves a particular value arising from her talent, before and after marriage, for taking her part in a duet. In contrast to words, which have wholly become signs, woman has remained at once a sign and a value. This explains why the relations between the sexes have preserved that affective richness, ardour and mystery which doubtless originally permeated the entire universe of human communications."[13]

Notes

1. C. Lévi-Strauss, *The Elementary Structures of Kinship*, translated by James Harle Bell, John Richard von Sturmer and Rodney Needham, Boston, Beacon Press, 1969, p. 8.
2. C. Lévi-Strauss, *Structural Anthropology*, translated by Claire Jacobson and Brooke Grundfest Schoepf, New York, Basic Books, 1963, p. 83.
3. Ibid., pp. 39–41.
4. A. R. Radcliffe-Brown, *Structure and Function in Primitive Society*, London, Cohen and West, 1952, pp. 15–31.
5. Lévi-Strauss, *Structural Anthropology*, p. 45.
6. Lévi-Strauss, *The Elementary Structures of Kinship*, p. 287.
7. R. Needham, *Structure and Sentiment: A Test Case in Social Anthropology*, Chicago, University of Chicago Press, 1962, pp. 17 and 115.
8. Ibid., pp. 8–10.
9. Lévi-Strauss, *The Elementary Structures of Kinship*, pp. xxx–xxxii.
10. R. Needham (ed.), *Rethinking Kinship and Marriage*, London, Tavistock, 1971.
11. P. Bourdieu, *The Logic of Practice*; translated from the French: *Le Sens practique*, Paris, Minuit, 1980, p. 272.
12. R. Deliège, *The World of the Untouchables: Paraiyars of Tamil Nadu*, translated by David Philips, Delhi, Oxford University Press, 1997; translated from the French: *Les Paraiyars du Tamil Nadu*, Fribourg, Presses Universitaires de Fribourg, 1998.
13. Lévi-Strauss, *The Elementary Structures of Kinship*, p. 496.

Part V
Symbolic Classifications

–1–

Totemism

In certain respects, Lévi-Strauss' work seems to come from another age, it has a nineteenth-century flavor. One finds relatively few references to recent studies, and he prefers to rely on the "classics". It is perhaps for this reason that the great traditional themes feature among his main preoccupations. This is the case of totemism, which the nineteenth-century authors saw as a fundamental stage in the development of human societies, to the point that it was said that totemism, like radar, whisky and marmalade, was invented by the Scots.

Classification

A Cognitive Approach

In *The Savage Mind*,[1] Lévi-Strauss writes that social anthropology is first of all a "psychology". Coming from someone who calls himself a sociologist, this claim may seem surprising. Yet in *Totemism*, Lévi-Strauss sets himself apart from Durkheim: the latter maintained the primacy of the social over the intellect, with categories and abstract ideas deriving from the social order.[2] For the father of French sociology, then, religious ideas are the product of the society, the expression of group solidarity. Structuralism does not accept this concept and considers, on the contrary, that it is the categories of thought, of the human mind, that create and construct reality. It is in this sense that Lévi-straussian anthropology leans towards a cognitive psychology of sorts, or a theory of the categories of the human mind.

From the 1960s, the bulk of his work would tend in this

direction with his studies on symbolic classification and mythology; the latter being also understood as indicative of the "mind's architecture". A society is regarded as a "set of symbolic systems", and symbolization as the primary activity of the human mind.[3] The mind is conceived as having objective reality, even if it is not actually defined. Contrary to the pure cognitivists, who start with the human "brain", Lévi-Strauss does not really look at the individual, but more at representations of a collective nature. The human mind is a sort of super-brain or collective brain. Empirical phenomena are thus merely concrete manifestations of what is possible, or realizations of the intrinsic capacities of the human mind. And one of the essential features of mind is classification.

Lévi-Strauss does not succumb to a pure idealism that denies reality, however. Reality exists, it is present, but it is simply the raw material, the inchoate mass in need of being taken in hand by the human mind in order to mean something.

The Illusion of Totemism

Contrary to what the earliest anthropologists thought, the notion of totemism does not denote a coherent body of phenomena. It is part of a whole, of the much broader problem of symbolic classifications, in other words, the way people bring order to their world. For evolutionists, totemic practices point to the archaic character of those primitive societies barely emerging from the state of nature, of which totemic groups are a remnant. Nevertheless, it would soon become apparent that the phenomena arbitrarily lumped together under the label of "totemism" did not constitute a homogeneous class: it is a disembodied notion, entirely devoid of substance.

It was an error to look for the key to totemism in the tie between the individual or the group and their totem. Among the Ojibwas, for instance, this tie is not seen as a relationship of contiguity. At best it can be metaphorical. The Ojibwas are not conscious of any zoological or botanical association. Contrary to what has been said, members of the bear clan do not take themselves for bears, no more than the myths establish a direct link between the animal species and the human group. Nor is the eponymous animal worshipped; it can be killed or eaten without any ritual precautions. Among the Tikopias studied by Firth, the animal is not seen either as an emblem or as an ancestor or in a relation of kinship. There is therefore not homology between the group and its totem either.

Totemic relations do not serve to establish a tie between a group and its totem, but rather to think a set of cultural features along the lines of a set of natural features. What matters is not the relationship between clan A and its totem, but that the relations between clans A, B, C … can be understood as relations between species in nature. What is usually meant by totemism is therefore only a way of manifesting a relationship between two series, one of which is natural and the other cultural.

Totemism and Exogamy

The link between totemism and exogamy is far from being as clear as some have claimed. Elkin's work on totemism in Australia has unearthed some particularly varied and complex situations. For instance, among the Aranda, exogamy is associated with the "subsections", which are completely independent from the totemic clans. And individual totems are found more or less everywhere. Elsewhere, as among the Murngin, the sections and subsections are totemic, but do not regulate marriage. In other terms, nothing is to be gained from looking to the organization of marriage or kinship for the origins or the essence of totemism.

Towards the Mind

From Durkheim to Social Anthropology

For Durkheim, the totem is a clan symbol. It expresses clan solidarity, which it represents in somewhat the same manner as the flag, national anthems, kings and presidents symbolize nations. To say that a totem is something sacred amounts to saying that there is a connection between the group and a natural species.

Durkheim's theory, as Radcliffe-Brown notes, does not explain why it is natural species that are chosen as symbols for the group. Moreover, it accounts for the solidarity of the totemic group, usually a clan, but says nothing about the society as a whole. Yet totemism not only expresses the clans' solidarity, it creates a connection between all the clans and establishes a homology between society and nature. Nevertheless, Radcliffe-Brown posits some link between the group and its totem: an animal does not become a totem unless it is good to eat. This is a case of "naive utilitarianism", which is invalidated by numerous examples.

Evans-Pritchard and Fortes were to take a decisive step when they looked at totemism as a comparison between two orders. The Nuers classify the animal kingdom according to social categories. In 1951, Radcliffe-Brown would revise his theory by recognizing structural analogies.

The Philosophers' Contribution

In order to gain a true understanding of totemism, it is necessary to go beyond an empiricism, that is beyond seeking an explanation in the facts. In reality totemism is merely an illustration of a certain way of thinking. It is therefore pointless to regard it as a phenomenon typical of a particularly archaic stage of evolution. It is a response to preoccupations of an intellectual order.

Thus a philosopher like Bergson had a better perception than anthropologists of what lies behind totemism. Rather than looking for an explanation in the pile of facts, his mind entered into resonance with the mind of the totemic group. He asserts that the members of two totemic clans emphasize their duality, and the difference between the two clans. This being the case, Lévi-Strauss comments, "It is not the resemblances, but the differences, which resemble each other".[4] Rousseau had clearly seen that social differentiation could be a lived experience only on the condition that it could be conceived.[5]

Totemism draws its conceptual basis for social differentiation from the diversity of the natural species.

Systems of Differences

Totemism is only one of the early manifestations of symbolic thinking, and a way for people to express their many different ways of living. The shift from nature to culture is also a shift from the animal state to the human state and, lastly, from affectivity to intellectuality. Totemism is thus a way of expressing this shift. Finally what it does is not so much say that a given clan resembles a given animal, but rather that two clans differ in the same way as two animal species; they are of different blood, while being of the same order. Nature and culture are thus conceived as two systems of differences between which a formal analogy exists that has to do with their systemic character: social groups are separate from each other, but they are bound together by ties of solidarity.

Totemism calls upon a homology not between social groups and natural species, but between two systems of differences: clan A is different from clan B in the same way as the bear is different from the eagle. Nature and culture are thus conceived in terms of systems of differences.

In the final analysis, *Totemism* shows that the primitive mind proceeds by understanding and not by affectivity. This would also be the theme of *The Savage Mind*, which will be examined in the next chapter.

Rethinking Primitivity

"We must therefore alter our traditional picture of this primitiveness. The 'savage' has certainly never borne any resemblance either to that creature barely emerged from an animal condition and still a prey to his needs and instincts who has so often been imagined nor to that consciousness governed by emotions and lost in a maze of confusion and participation."[6]

–2–

The Savage Mind

In this chapter we will look more closely at *The Savage Mind*, a work published in the same year as *Totemism*, with which it is closely linked. In *The Savage Mind* the reflection becomes more general and to a certain extent can be seen as part of the discussion on modes of thought and the primitive mind.

Beyond the Primitive Mind

Lévy-Bruhl

The French philosopher Lévy-Bruhl spent his life studying ways of thinking. Briefly put, he maintains that the primitive mind differs profoundly from the "civilized" mind and that it can be described as "prelogical", for primitive man has a mystical perception of the universe.[7] Lévy-Bruhl stands apart from the other evolutionists, who think that whatever is simplest is the earliest in time. What interests him is the dichotomy between two modes of thought, namely prelogical thought and rational thought. The collective representations of primitive peoples, he emphasizes, do not have a logical, rational character. For them everything has mystical properties: objects, for example, have a mystical, non-material existence. The Indians of Guyana refuse to improve on their tools because they fear that in doing so they might alter their invisible mystical properties; for the primitive man, these mystical properties have as much importance as their material reality: a man's shadow, for example, is considered by the Fiji Islanders to be his soul, and Cherokee Indians seek treatment when they dream of having been bitten by a snake. For the primitive man, there is no opposition between the physical world and the mystical world, and in this case mystical action supplants natural law. The natural and the supernatural are not separate for primitive peoples; there is only one world. Their mode of thought is governed by a law of participation between the physical and the mystical worlds.

Such is the thrust of Lévy-Bruhl's thesis. Contrary to a criticism sometimes advanced, he does not say that primitive man is irrational or illogical, but rather that his manner of thinking is prelogical. Nevertheless, he also says that primitive peoples do not think rationally, and that their mind does not obey the same laws as "ours"; the way "lower" societies think is therefore not altogether impenetrable, but it is not altogether intelligible either.

The Savage Scientist

Lévi-Strauss refuses to see the savage as a non-rational being. On the contrary, he presents him as an eminently rational being, and only a sophisticated analysis can manage to seize the complexity of his mind. "In the face of such accuracy and care one begins to wish that every anthropologist were also a mineralogist, a botanist, a zoologist and even an astronomer".[8] Indigenous classifications are not only methodical and based "on carefully built up theoretical knowledge. They are also at times comparable from a formal point of view, to those still in use in zoology and botany."[9]

In other words, the savage is a man of science. To be sure, his is a special kind of science, but he uses conceptual tools and thinking processes comparable to those of civilized man, and even of the best scientists. One sees how Lévi-Strauss' savage is created in his own image: on the one hand, he is a being bound by ties of solidarity to the other members of a social organization founded on exchange. And on the other hand, he justifies our admiration by proving to be a top-notch intellectual, since even Neolithic man is "the heir of a long scientific tradition".[10] In short, he is something of a democratic scientist, one could almost say a "left-wing intellectual".

It is pointless to isolate the savage from the civilized man. To understand him, one must enter into his way of thinking. This "savage mind" is not that of an archaic or primitive stage of mankind, but, on the contrary, "a mind in the savage state", distinct from the mind that has been "cultivated or domesticated for the purpose of yielding a return".[11] In other words, thanks to primitive societies, we have access to a pure, uncorrupted mode of thought.

Classificatory Logic

The Savage Mind thus analyzes the workings of the mind in its pure state: a mind attempting to bring order to the world, to make it coherent.

The Science of the Concrete

The savage world is not governed by needs or instincts, but on the contrary, by requirements of an intellectual order. The savage mind is concerned with setting the universe in order. This demand for order is a fundamental feature: each thing must be in its proper place, and any kind of classification at all is better than chaos. The discoveries of the Neolithic era suppose many centuries of active, methodical observation. The need for method and classification are as characteristic of the primitive world as they are of our own thinking.

In primitive society, the savage mind can use only that which it has at hand. Like the handyman who makes use of whatever is lying around, the savage mind is forced to use leftovers, bits and pieces, but that by no means stands in the way of achieving brilliant results. Savage thinking is a science of the concrete, a practical science or a kind of technology but a science nonetheless, in the sense that it organizes the perceptible world. The very function of myth is to work out structured arrangements using the material at hand. Allegorical language is merely a façade that conceals a profound abstract thinking process; the myth constructs a whole:

> Several thousand Coahuila Indians never exhausted the natural resources of a desert region in South California, in which today only a handful of white families manage to subsist. They lived in a land of plenty, for in this apparently completely barren territory, they were familiar with no less than sixty kinds of edible plants and twenty-eight others of narcotic, stimulant or medicinal properties … A single Seminol informant could identify two hundred and fifty species and varieties of plants … Three hundred and fifty plants known to the Hopi Indians and more than five hundred to the Navaho have been recorded.[12]

Nothing is left to chance in the utilization of natural species. Totemic classifications include birds by virtue of certain features, or of their semantic position within the culture, which demands a thorough knowledge on the part of the analyst, who must grapple with considerable difficulties.

From Totem to Caste

The logical principle of classificatory thought is always the setting of one term against another; these terms constitute convertible codes. One can think that there is a basic analogy between *totemic societies* and *caste-based societies*. In both cases, each group performs a specialized function indispensable to the group as a whole: the Aboriginal tribes of Australia assign a separate magical-religious function to each totemic group. The apparently radical opposition between totem and caste can therefore be called into doubt. On the contrary, it can be thought that they are closely related, and that they are different expressions of the same thought mechanisms.

In the case of totemism, as we have seen, we are dealing with homology between two systems of differences. In a clan society, clan 1 differs from clan 2 as the bear differs from the eagle. Culture and nature are considered to be two systems of differences. The social groups are seen as being different, but bound by ties of solidarity, they are envisaged as forming a system.

Nature	species 1	≠	species 2	≠	species 3	≠	species 4
Culture	group 1	≠	group 2	≠	group 3	≠	group 4

A society that rejects solidarity between its social groups becomes a caste-based society. In this case, each group is envisaged in its own right, and the emphasis then falls on the group's relations with a reality of another order: group 1 becomes the bear, group 2 becomes the eagle, and so forth.

Nature	species 1	species 2	species 3	species 4
	=	=	=	=
Culture	group 1	group 2	group 3	group 4

There is thus a shift from an *exo-praxis* (turning outward) to an *endo-praxis* (turning inward). This endo-praxis appears when it comes to kinship, for castes are ostensibly endogamous, while clans are exogamous. Many castes in South India do not have natural species as totems but rather artifacts: scissors, house, boat, coin, etc. It is as though the totemic groups in this case were envisaged with culture in mind: all these differentiated objects are not seen in terms of a natural order. The parallel between the two systems of differences has disappeared: the stress here is placed on the link between the object and the group.

In Answer to Sartre

In the final chapters of *The Savage Mind*, Lévi-Strauss speaks directly to Jean-Paul Sartre, who was indisputably a *monstre sacré* of the French intelligentsia at the time. From that point on, Lévi-Strauss would be seen as a sort of rival. He strongly rejects Sartre's conception of history, which he deems ethnocentric, and the central position he attributes to man, to whom he opposes structure, while edging history out of the field of anthropology.[13]

The characteristic feature of the savage mind is its timelessness; its

> object is to grasp the world as both a synchronic and a diachronic totality … It builds mental structures which facilitate an understanding of the world … In this sense, savage thought can be defined as analogical thought.[14]

In the final analysis, *The Savage Mind* returns to the criticism of progress already present in *Tristes Tropiques* or in *Race and History*.

–3–

The Effectiveness of Symbols

If there is one domain that has always been regarded as a mark of archaic thinking, it is surely that of magic and sorcery. For Lévi-Strauss, however, these are not a sign of traditionalism, but once again the expression of a mode of thought found as much in modern societies as in those that belong to the field of classical ethnological studies. In two influential texts published in *Structural Anthropology* ("The Sorcerer and His Magic" and "The Effectiveness of Symbols"),[15] Lévi-Strauss dismantles the mechanisms of this thinking: in his view, they oddly resemble those of the psychoanalytical cure. Once again the savage, a veritable therapist, is transformed into a scholar.

The Sorcerer and his Magic

Belief

There is no reason to doubt the effectiveness of certain magical practices. But how does this apparently occult effectiveness fit with the rationalization of the savage mind that Lévi-Strauss has elevated to the status of a principle? For the anthropologist cannot accept that there are supernatural forces capable of healing. The explanation must lie elsewhere, and so Lévi-Strauss transforms the sorcerer into a sort of psychoanalyst.

Magic, he says, presupposes belief. For magic to work, for it to be effective, one must believe in it. In other words it could be said that one must penetrate a world of meaning. Belief entails three aspects: the sorcerer's belief in the effectiveness of his techniques; the patient's or victim's belief in the sorcerer's power; and lastly, the belief of the group. Magic and sorcery rest on a coherent system of integrated beliefs that converge upon a single outcome. The use of magic calls for a consensus that is difficult to avoid.

The Power of Words

Using a study by an American anthropologist, Lévi-Strauss investigates the sociological or psychological mechanisms at work in cases of death by curse or bewitching. When an individual becomes aware that he has been the object of sorcery or cursed, he is intimately persuaded by the tradition of his group that he is doomed. From that moment on, the community stands aloof; they avoid the accursed man, and treat him as though he were already dead. And thus he is doomed to die. Cut off from family, excluded from society, his physical integrity cannot survive the disintegration of his personality. For Lévi-Strauss, then, it is the ostracism from society that explains the death.

The indigenous formula "spell => death", becomes for Lévi-Strauss "spell => social exclusion => death". The advantage of the new formula is that it minimizes the effect of a supernatural element. In line with Durkheim, it is natural to die of ostracism, and the explanation is now sociologically acceptable. And yet one wonders what has been gained. The magical belief has simply become a sociological belief, for there is still no explanation of how ostracism leads to death, unless it is a sort of belief in the absolute powers of psychosomatic reactions, that is to say the transformation of an idea into a physical problem.

Abreaction

For Lévi-Strauss a man does not become a sorcerer because he heals the sick, he heals the sick because he has become a sorcerer. Belief therefore precedes effectiveness.

In the shamanistic cure, the shaman* relives the original crisis whereby his vocation was revealed to him. In psychoanalytical theory, "abreaction" is the decisive moment when the patient intensely relives the initial situation at the root of his disturbance before going on to overcome his problem. One could thus consider the shaman as a sort of professional "abre-actor": through his trances he can symbolically induce the patient's own disorder. In other words, Lévi-Strauss suggests that, by watching the shaman relive his initial trance experience, the patient too becomes able to relive the original circumstances of his illness and thereby be almost miraculously cured.

This would make the shaman no more than a sort of proto-psychoanalyst. But, once again, it is hard to see what we have gained by this explanation. The process of abreaction is already problematic in itself; now we have to accept the idea that seeing someone else relive intense emotions can suffice to resolve one's own conflicts. Whatever the case may be, we are still in the realm of belief. And the psychoanalytical vocabulary adds nothing. One wonders whether, in wanting to make the shaman into a sort of psychoanalyst, Lévi-Strauss has not made the latter into a sort of magician. Is it enough to believe for the magic to work?

The Shaman's Cure

The parallel between the shamanistic "cure" and psychoanalysis is developed in the text entitled "The Effectiveness of Symbols". The article is based on material collected by Warner and Holmer among the Cuna Indians of Panama. In it there is a reference to a song or incantation used in the event of difficult childbirth. It is seldom utilized, only in rare cases in which the midwife proves to be powerless

The Magical Incantation

The text says that Muu, the power responsible for forming the fetus, has made away with the *purba*, the soul of the mother-to-be. The incantation is a search for the lost *purba*, which will eventually be restored after an eventful quest (obstacles, combat with ferocious animals, etc.). Vanquished, Muu frees the soul and the child can be born. In order to find Muu, the shaman and his helpers must follow a path: Muu's road.

The battle with the spirits occupies only a small part of the incantation. Alternatively, the preliminaries are developed at length. Particular emphasis is placed on the conversation between the midwife and the woman in labor, past events, the shaman's arrival, etc. It is as though the officiant were trying to get the patient to relive intensely an initial situation and to visualize every single detail. The aim of the incantation seems to be to describe to the sick woman not only the facts, but also all the fantastic monsters and animals that haunt her in a world straight out of Hieronymous Bosch.

The Cure

According to this theory, then, the cure consists of enabling the patient to conceive a situation first of all in terms of affects, but also to enable the mind to accept the pains that the body refuses to tolerate. It does not matter whether or not the shaman's myth corresponds to objective reality. The patient believes and is a member of a society that believes. The protecting and the harmful spirits, the monsters and other magical animals are all part of a coherent system underpinning the natural order of the world. What the patient does not accept are the incoherent and arbitrary pains that are alien to her system.

And so the patient gets well. In societies such as Levi-Strauss' own, evocation of the cause of their disturbance, germs or viruses, is not enough to cure patients, for the relationship between the germs and the patient is external to the patient's mind. For the Cuna, on the other hand, the relationship between the monster and the human mind is internal to the mind. It is a relation of *signifié* to *signifiant*, of symbol to the thing symbolized, which are two aspects of the same phenomenon. In this case, Lévi-Strauss affirms that, by acting on one, one acts on the other: the recourse to verbal expression here too triggers the physiological process.

The shamanistic cure goes even further than the psychoanalytical cure since it resolves physiological problems. Like psychoanalysis, though, it raises to the conscious level the conflicts and resistances that were lurking in the unconscious. In effect, the woman in labor overcomes a true organic disorder by identifying with the shaman.

Critique

The first problem that Lévi-Strauss' explanation poses is the extent to which the case examined is representative, since it is so particular that one does not see how it can be considered typical of shamanistic practice. Furthermore, Lévi-Strauss asserts that the cathartic value of the therapy in question resides in the penetrating action of the words. Yet specialists in Cuna culture have affirmed that the shaman's incantation is esoteric and that the patient does not understand it. It is therefore hard to accept that the words alone are enough to raise a conflict to the conscious level.

Even if the words were understood, one docs not see how words spoken by someone else, even a magician, can resolve an organic problem. Furthermore, in many cases the patient is not even present. And when this is the case, the patient is sometimes asleep or unconscious. More often the shaman confronts the demons on his own, without any participation whatsoever on the part of the patient. And there is never any question of past events.

Lévi-Strauss' analysis rests on nothing more than conjecture. He has reduced a spiritual process to psychobabble, which is clearly more acceptable to the readers of *Structural Anthropology*, the bulk of whom do not believe in the effectiveness of telluric forces. Once again one must ask what the analysis has gained in the process. It is not based on any empirical evidence. Contrary to what Lévi-Strauss suggests, the shaman does not claim to heal broken bones or cure cancer or blindness on the strength of words alone. To assert that a myth (the shaman's incantation) can produce organic changes (a successful birth) is tantamount to a belief of the same order as recourse to evil spirits. Whatever concerns illness, anxiety and death often goes beyond purely rational explanations. But to believe that traditional groups claim to resolve everything through shamanistic practices comes down to confining them to a primitive prerational way of thinking.[16]

Notes

1. C. Lévi-Strauss, *The Savage Mind*, Chicago, University of Chicago Press, 1969 [no translator mentioned].
2. C. Lévi-Strauss, *Totemism*, translated by Rodney Needham, London, Penguin, 1969, p. 77.
3. C. Lévi-Strauss, *Introduction to the Work of Marcel Mauss*, translated by Felicity Baker, London, Routledge and Kegan Paul, 1987, p. 48–9.
4. Lévi-Strauss, *Totemism*, p. 77.
5. Lévi-Strauss, *Le Totémisme aujourd'hui*, Paris, Presses Universitaires de France, 1962, p. 145.
6. Lévi-Strauss, *The Savage Mind*, p. 42.
7. See e.g. L. Lévy-Bruhl, *How Natives Think*, translated by Lilian A. Clare, Princeton, Princeton University Press, 1985.
8. Lévi-Strauss, *The Savage Mind*, p. 44.
9. Ibid., p. 43.
10. Ibid., p. 15.
11. Ibid., p. 219.
12. Ibid., p. 5.
13. Ibid., p. 256.
14. Ibid., p. 263.
15. For the rest of this chapter, see C. Lévi-Strauss, *Structural Anthropology*, translated by Claire Jacobson and Brooke Grundfest Schoepf, New York, Basic Books, 1963, pp. 167–205.
16. For a criticism of this viewpoint, see e.g. J. Atkinson, "The Effectiveness of Shamanism in an Indonesian Ritual", *The American Anthropologist*, 89, 1987, pp. 342–55.

Part VI
Mythology

–1–

The Basis of Myths

The Importance of Studying Myths

A Vast Undertaking

After the publication of *The Savage Mind*, Lévi-Strauss devoted a good part of his time to the study of myths. The outcome was four large volumes grouped together under the general title of *Introduction to a Science of Mythology.* Once again, these were greeted as an event and widely discussed in numerous intellectual circles. This was particularly the case with the first two volumes, *The Raw and the Cooked*, and *From Honey to Ashes*, which seemed like models of analysis. With erudition and sophistication, the author succeeds in introducing us to the world of American Indian tribes, giving us the impression that it was possible thereby to resolve crucial philosophical problems that had not ceased to haunt us. *The Origin of Table Manners* and *Naked Man*, the last two volumes, met with less success; no doubt readers felt they knew enough about the problem, but in reality their patience may also have been tried by so much detail.

At the risk of appearing iconoclastic, I do not feel that these works are really essential. Sometimes they even verge on intellectual pedantry, and one could ask oneself whether it is still of any use to read them. The myth analyses that are repeated in *Structural Anthropology* and *Structural Anthropology II*, for example the "Story of Aswidal", are in this sense appreciably more operational and just as informative as the analytical overdose in the four big volumes. In spite of these reservations, however, many aspects of Lévi-Strauss' analysis still deserve our attention.

Why Myths?

The study of myths is a direct extension of the earlier works. The aim is to show that there is indeed such a thing as mythic thought or, at least, a mythic manner of thinking. Everywhere in the world people relate myths, that is to say allegorical accounts meant to explain the origin of their institutions. Such a universal phenomenon poses a question; it cannot be a matter of chance or cultural exchanges. If myths are found the world over, it is because they express a way of thinking characteristic of all humans: they partake of the laws of the mind's structure.[1] The laws governing the way myths operate are the same as those governing the human mind.

Everything would seem simple if, in *The Raw and the Cooked*, Lévi-Strauss had not made this statement, which is mysterious to say the least: "I therefore claim to show, not how men think in myths, but how myths operate [literally: 'think themselves'] in men's minds without their being aware of the fact."[2] The meaning of this clarification is not clear to me: how can myths be considered to "think"? It could also be said that the myth is not the expression of a specific thought, of a reflection, but that it expresses mechanisms. Perhaps Lévi-Strauss would prefer myths to exist without men? But that cannot be, for without a narrator there is no myth, whatever Lévi-Strauss may say. We will also see that he tends to make the myth too independent of its conditions of production so that it becomes an object in itself, capable of existing without a subject.

An Innovative Approach

Earlier Theories

The functional theories of myths place them in the sociological context of their emergence. Myths play a role in maintaining the social order; they express social realities and are therefore closely connected with reality. For psychoanalysis, myths enact fundamental conflicts in the psyche. Others search myths for fragments of history, traces of the past of the societies that relate them. Each time, the myth is reduced to another reality.

The Myth in Itself

According to Lévi-Strauss, on the contrary, the myth is a reality *sui generis*, that can, and must, be studied in and for itself, without reference to a context, whether historical, psychological or sociological. Myths "are the very exercise of the savage mind. Their internal unity, their logical consistency therefore do not lie in their likelihood or in their referent".[3] It is as though, for Lévi-Strauss, myths existed for themselves, and were not bound up with the peoples or the persons who relate them. Everything must be explained myth by myth. The myth is a closed reality.[4] The myth does not talk about something, it is a category of mind, and the primary and deepest expression of the thinking process.[5] One might wonder whether, in taking this line, Lévi-Strauss does not himself become part of a sort of myth of structure and structuralism.

The myth is an incoherent account: anything can happen in a myth, and the sequence of events does not seem to obey any rule of logic or continuity. Extraordinary things become ordinary: birds have sexual intercourse with humans, heroes ascend into the sky, fish smoke pipes, children are born from fruits or rivers, animals talk and act like humans. For Lévi-Strauss, there is a hidden meaning behind all this non-sense, and, once again, the message of the myth usually has to do with the resolution of a contradiction.

Transformations

The same myth has various known versions, and this diversity has always been a problem for interpretation. According to Lévi-Strauss, within a given cultural zone, the different versions of the same myth form a system.[6] By superposing these different versions, it becomes possible to grasp the underlying structure. On the scale of linguistic modes of expression, Lévi-Strauss explains, myth is at the opposite end from poetry. Poetry does not tolerate the slightest transformation: its form must imperatively remain unchanged. It is altogether another matter for myth, the form of which varies constantly: from one narrator to the next, one generation to the next, the form of the myth changes, but what the analysis is supposed to show is its "structure", that which remains unchanged in spite of the countless versions. Myths can be told in different ways: they can be summarized, paraphrased or translated without altering their value.

It is perhaps in this sense that we can speak of "the" Œdipus myth or "the" Don Juan myth, despite the many versions to be found the world over. In reality, the myth is unaltered by these variations, and it is up to the analysis to reveal its structure. Finally, there is no reason to privilege one version over another; on the contrary, variations bring out the significant elements.

An Example

The Origin of Fire

These few principles can be illustrated by an example.[7] Certain American Indian myths recount the origin of the cooking fire. They describe a bird-nester hero who is stuck up a tree or on a rocky cliff side following a quarrel with a brother-in-law. He is delivered by a jaguar and, after some adventures, comes back to his kinsmen with the fire of which the jaguar was master. It also turns out that the jaguar is married to a woman and is therefore an ally of human beings.

Another group of myths relates the origin of meat. This time they tell of superhuman heroes who are at odds with the men to whom they are related by marriage. The men refuse to give them the food that is theirs by right as givers of women. To punish them, the heroes turn them into wild pigs.

The analysis consists in reducing the myth to systems of oppositions. In the first group of myths, for example, two characteristic relations can be seen: (1) human hero/jaguar and (2) benevolent animal/man. In the second group these relations become: (1) superhuman hero/man and (2) malevolent man/animal. The man is sometimes a hero, sometimes a victim. The benevolent figure becomes malevolent. Proceeding in this fashion, it is possible to discover systems of oppositions at various levels, for instance, culinary, cosmological, sociological, etc.

The elements are not seen in themselves, but as terms of opposition: thus it does not matter whether, depending on the version, the hero is perched in a tree or on the side of a cliff; what matters is, of course, that he is in an elevated position and therefore that high is opposed to low. At the culinary level there is an opposition between raw meat and cooked meat, and the appearance of fire ensures the movement from one to the other. At the cosmological level there is an opposition between total conjunction of the Sun and the Earth (which would result in a burned earth) and total disjunction (which would result in a rotted earth).

Continuing the analysis, it is possible to see a common pattern: in different forms, the myths studied tell of the establishment and the meaning of culture as mediator between (infra-human) nature and the (supra-human) sacred realm. In other words, these myths succeed in resolving a problem, and even a basic contradiction. Through them, people come to understand themselves as intermediary beings, as being rooted in nature, but at the same time capable of instituting an order of rules other than that of nature. In myth we define ourselves as cultural beings.

From One Order to the Other

The myth is systematically chopped up into segments, which Lévi-Strauss calls "mythemes" (referring to the "phonemes" of language).[8] These segments carry a meaning that is different from their primary sense. They need to be reduced to oppositions (high/low, raw/cooked, human/animal, etc.). The immediate order of the account should not be followed, but instead the elements grouped according to the "levels" or "orders": sociological (marriage, clan …), techno-culinary, cosmological, etc. Then a meaning common to all these different systems of oppositions should be sought.

From Shakespeare to Perrault

In a recent book,[9] the anthropologist Dan Sperber showed that, with a little ingenuity, everything can be reduced to opposites.

Hamlet	*Little Red Ridinghood*
Male hero	Female hero
Clashes with his mother	Obeys her mother
Meets a supra-human being	Meets an infra-human being
That is frightening	That is reassuring
But has good intentions	But has bad intentions
And urges him to hurry	And urges her to dally
etc.	etc.

Can it be that the absurdity of such a construction stems from the fact that these stories are familiar to us whereas the remoteness of the Bororo seems to authorize far bolder associations?

–2–

The Raw, the Cooked, Honey and Ashes

In the previous chapter, I outlined the main principles of Lévi-Strauss' approach to the study of mythology. We will now look at how these general ideas were put into practice by examining a few specific studies.

The Science of Mythology

Lévi-Strauss refuses, as it were, to admit that there can be any form of thought other than that which governs science. It is for this reason that he attempts to reduce all activities of "savages" to solutions that are logical and, even more than rational, perfectly scientific. Let us take the example of Volume One of his *Introduction to a Science of Mythology, The Raw and the Cooked*. In eruditely decoding in minute detail these rather fantastic stories that make up the myths of Latin American tribes, Lévi-Strauss intends to demonstrate that "the apparent arbitrariness of the mind, its supposedly spontaneous flow of inspiration, and its seemingly uncontrolled inventiveness imply the existence of laws operating at a deeper level",[10] he speaks of a "science of myths",[11] which is still in its infancy but of which he is proposing some preliminary results here. The human mind, he goes on to say, "appears determined even in the realm of mythology".[12] Mythology exists independently of time and place; it is even an "instrument for the obliteration of time".[13] Myths also exist independently of the persons who recount them, and who merely multiply the versions leaving the structure intact, since it is not available to the conscious mind; therefore in order to understand myths, one must disregard the subject.

An Ojibwa Myth

An Ojibwa myth tells, for example, how the gods put an end to the proliferation of humans: the latter were supposed to present a gift to the god Akaruio Bokodori; the god approved the gifts of the members of five clans only, and all the others were put to death by bow and arrow.

If one accepts the existence of clans bearing insignificant gifts, there is a risk that an unlimited number of other clans or other peoples might present themselves alongside them, differing so little from their neighbors that they would all ultimately merge into each other. Humans therefore had to become less numerous; the quantity had to be limited in order that a coherent system of significances might be constructed.[14] Lévi-Strauss goes further still: the Ojibwa gods who organize the reduction of men to a few simple classes, he notes, are blind. Akaruio Bokodori has a limp, as does another hero in the myth: this reference to infirmities, Lévi-Strauss believes, makes possible the changeover from an infinite world to a discrete world. Indeed it is possible to achieve finitude only by subtracting, destroying or removing something from the original order. Therefore the authors of such impoverishments are themselves diminished beings. “Mythological figures who are blind or lame, one-eyed or one-armed, are familiar the world over; and we find them disturbing, because we believe their condition to be one of deficiency. But just as a system that has been made discrete through the removal of certain elements becomes logically richer, although numerically poorer, so myths often confer a positive significance on the disabled and the sick, who embody modes of mediation. We imagine infirmity and sickness to be deprivations of being and therefore evil. However, if death is as real as life, all states, even pathological ones, are positive in their own way. ‘Negativized being’ [literally: the state of ‘less being’] is entitled to occupy a whole place within the system, since it is the only conceivable means of transition between two ‘full’ states.”[15] Myths, he concludes, offer original solutions to the problem of the shift from continuous quantity to discrete quantity.

An Ontological Solution

But Lévi-Strauss does not quit while he is ahead. He sees this determination to resolve existential tensions everywhere. He comments on a Bororo myth in the following terms: "Everything is therefore interrelated: tobacco smoke engenders wild pigs, which supply meat. In order that this meat may be roasted, a bird-nester has to obtain cooking fire from the jaguar; finally, to get rid of the jaguar, another bird-nester has to burn its corpse on a fire, thus causing the birth of tobacco."[16]

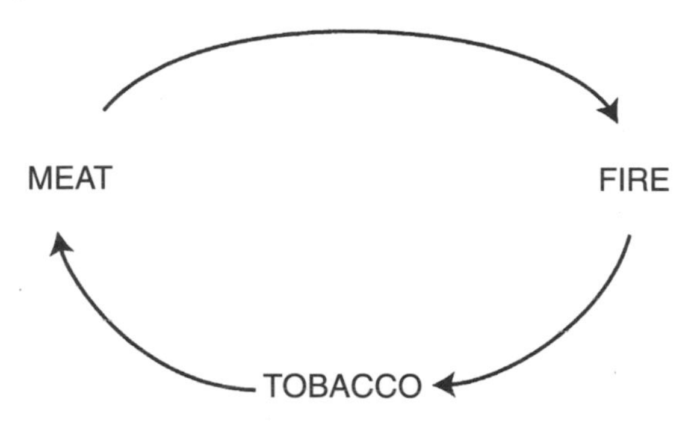

The savage lives here in a sophisticated world of logical systems. Behind the apparent aberration of allegorical and phantasmagoric details lies an implacable logic, and a whole system of cause and effect that brings us back to a veritable system of dialectics. The savage's world is a forerunner of the debates that animate the most famous philosophers' works: he spends his time solving "logical problems", even if he often does this in the allegorical language of myth. For instance, the founding agricultural myths feature the opossum, a small, foul-smelling, inedible marsupial; just as decay is the opposite of the edible plant, so the non-edible opossum personifies an anti-agriculture: "the mediatory function of the opossum … offers a midway solution to the philosophical problems arising from the introduction of an agricultural mode of life."[17] The anthropologist's role is to bring out this deep logic: everything has a meaning, nothing is left to chance, and "when a contradiction appears, it proves that the analysis has not been taken far enough".[18] In the end, the savage astonishes us by his intellectual sophistication. We are a long way here from Frazer's vision of a savage world enmeshed in illusory magical manipulations. The savage thinks like us, like the best of us; he is now a philosopher, a good one – a rationalist philosopher who cannot conceive the world without reason and logic, who must resolve a number of intolerable contradictions. The mental functions of primitive people, according to Lévi-Strauss, seem quite similar to our own. Mythical thought, he concludes, in *The Savage Mind,* "can reach brilliant … results on the intellectual plane".[19]

The sociologist Pierre Bourdieu rightly denounced the excesses of this approach in *The Logic of Practice*:

> No doubt because they know and recognize no other thought than the thought of the "thinker", and cannot grant human dignity without granting what seems to be constitutive of that dignity, anthropologists have never known how to rescue the people they were studying from the barbarism of the pre-logic except by identifying them with the most prestigious of their colleagues – logicians or philosophers.[20]

By thus making the primitive man into a refined intellectual, Lévi-Strauss assuredly contributed to the formidable enthusiasm that surrounded anthropology, but he also somewhat misrepresented the human mind by reducing it to a machine for making logical rules. There is no room in his explanations for emotion, wonder, joy, sorrow and love. And, though myths can explain some things, one wonders if their primary reason for existing is really intellectual. Furthermore, in spite of the obvious methodological interest of his reading and interpretation of myths, they sometimes resemble syllogisms in that learned constructs are built upon erroneous or arbitrary premises. As the American anthropologists Lynn Thomas and Judy and David Kronenfeld write, structural analysis only leads "into a world where all things are possible and nothing sure".[21]

The Story of Aswidal

It is in the study of myths more than anywhere else that Lévi-Strauss has used his favorite methodological tools, namely *synecdoche* and *antithesis*. Every aspect of reality is irremediably transformed by means of these procedures. Synecdoche is a rhetorical figure that consists in taking the part for the whole, more for less: it changes the pot into "container", water into "contained"; the moccasin treading the grass is reduced to an opposition between "culture" and "nature". When using antithesis, an element is considered only in relation to its opposite. The essential task of the analysis boils down to reducing the episodes and elements of the myth to all sorts of oppositions. The reader is sometimes literally left drowning in detail, and it is not always easy to find our way along the intellectual path that leads us from these mythical allegorics to abstract conclusions, to put it mildly. In *Introduction to a Science of Mythology*, in particular, the demonstration is so dense and meandering, it winds in and out of so many digressions and diagrams, that one is hard put to fault it. It is no doubt on that account, and not because of its intrinsic qualities or shortcomings, that Lévi-Strauss' shortest text, "The Story of Aswidal", has been the object of so many comments and critiques.

After having distinguished four "orders" (geographic, economic, sociological and cosmological), Lévi-Strauss remarks that the relationship between reality and myth is a complex one. At times the account reproduces reality, at times it contradicts reality. The logic of the myth should be sought more in the insurmountable oppositions with which Aswidal is confronted. His adventures can be seen as a series of mediations between these oppositions.

When one compares the various versions, one notices that every possible arrangement of elements seems to have been envisaged, such that the comparison reveals a set of transformations. The myth thus enumerates the extreme positions in order to demonstrate their untenable character. In the final analysis, it expresses a fundamental aspect of indigenous philosophy: namely that the only positive mode of being is a negation of non-being.[22]

Notes

1. C. Lévi-Strauss, *The Raw and the Cooked, Introduction to a Science of Mythology*, Volume 1, translated by John and Doreen Weightman, New York, Penguin, 1986, p. 10.
2. C. Lévi-Strauss, *The Raw and the Cooked*, p. 12.
3. M. Hénaff, *Claude Lévi-Strauss*, Paris, Belfond, 1991, p. 171.
4. D. Dubuisson, *Mythologies du XXe siècle (Dumézil, Lévi-Strauss, Eliade)*, Lille, Presses Universitaires de Lille, 1993, p. 151.
5. Ibid., p. 147.
6. C. Lévi-Strauss, *Structural Anthropology*, translated by Claire Jacobson and Brooke Grundfest Schoepf, New York, Basic Books, 1963, p. 218.
7. Lévi-Strauss, *The Raw and the Cooked*, p. 68.
8. Lévi-Strauss, *Structural Anthropology*, p. 210.
9. D. Sperber, *La Contagion des idées*, Paris, Odite Jacob, 1996, p. 66.
10. Lévi-Strauss, *The Raw and the Cooked*, p. 10.
11. Ibid., p. 3.
12. Ibid., p. 10.
13. Ibid., p. 16.
14. Ibid., p. 53.
15. Ibid., p. 53.
16. Ibid., p. 106.
17. Ibid., p. 186.
18. Ibid., p. 162.
19. C. Lévi-Strauss, *The Savage Mind*, Chicago, University of

Chicago Press, 1969 [no translator mentioned], p. 17.

20. P. Bourdieu, *The Logic of Practice*, translated by Richard Nice, Cambridge, UK, Polity Press 1990, p. 37.
21. L. Thomas, J. Kronenfeld and D. Kronenfeld, "Aswidal Crumbles: A Critique of Levi-Straussian Myth Analysis", *American Ethnologist*, 3, 1976, p. 150.
22. See C. Lévi-Strauss, "The Story of Aswidal", in Edmund Leach (ed.), *The Structural Study of Myth and Totemism*, London, Tavistock, 1967, pp. 1-48. For a critical appraisal, see Mary Douglas, "The Meaning of Myth with Special Reference to 'Le Geste d'Aswidal'", in Leach (ed.), *The Structural Study*, pp. 49–70.

Part VII
The Impact of Structuralism on Social Anthropology

In the social sciences, the great currents of thought exert two kinds of influence: a direct influence, particularly in the case of disciples who immediately comment on or apply the "master's" work; and a more subtle, indirect impact, more diffuse as well and sometimes more critical, but also sometimes more fruitful. The first kind is fairly short lived, often dying out with the dominant figures; the second is more enduring, but less easily identified; it permeates the work, and crops up everywhere, sometimes even in unexpected places.

–1–

The Development of French Anthropology

Towards a Noble Science

Although it is not always acknowledged, Lévi-Strauss had a considerable impact on the development of social anthropology in France, where he played a role comparable to that of Boas in the USA or Malinowski in Great Britain. Before him, French anthropology was something of a musty discipline that enjoyed much less prominence than it did in the UK or America. Outside of Durkheim and Mauss, one could hardly speak of a real French influence on anthropology and even less on ethnography. Lévi-Strauss' role was therefore a decisive one. In the first place, he made social anthropology into a noble and intellectually stimulating science. Whereas this discipline readily fell into a fairly rudimentary empiricism, Lévi-Strauss offered a new intellectual and theoretical program, and he opened avenues of investigation that were as unexplored as they were ambitious. At the time, functionalism* was no longer attracting younger researchers, probably because of its relative theoretical poverty. And Marxism was having difficulty imposing itself among anthropologists, who were hard put to consider that indigenous societies might be involved in history and class struggle. In short, structuralism, which was an incredible mixture of linguistics, philosophy and positivism, appeared as a (last) hope for a theoretical revival of the analysis of human societies.

Lévi-Strauss' rigor was as appealing as his creativity. His reasoning seemed impeccable, sometimes abstruse, to be sure, but always stimulating. He had an extraordinary capacity to make the "savage" seem at once familiar and essential, showing us that the problems he affronted and solved were by no means trivial. Social anthropology became a respectable discipline, it might even be said "fashionable" were there not the risk of discrediting the formidable enthusiasm that went far beyond a minor passing fancy. Indeed, Lévi-Strauss was to shape, directly or indirectly, a whole generation of researchers and give French research in anthropology a new lease of life. With Lévi-Strauss, France became a privileged center of research on indigenous cultures.

Lévi-Strauss quickly became a highly respected figure on the French intellectual stage. In fact, he was long regarded as France's *premier* intellectual. Although he did not take advantage of his huge prestige and remained rather modest, his was regarded as the authoritative word. In France for a long time any criticism of Lévi-Strauss appeared to be biased or, even worse, sacrilegious. Today, of course, passions have cooled, but much of his authority remains, and he continues to command respect, in particular for the formidable impetus he gave to social anthropology.

Enlargement of the Field of Study

Lévi-Strauss' anthropology transcended the relativistic particularisms in which social anthropology seemed to be mired. It not only went beyond empiricism, it also showed that the detour through primitive society was crucial to our understanding of society more broadly. One of his great merits was no doubt to have reminded us that anthropology talks about humankind, or that the questions it asks of the "savage" invariably bring us back to humankind in general. For Lévi-Strauss, social anthropology was a branch of empirical philosophy, and it furnished the demonstration of Rousseau's and Montaigne's theses. Social anthropology was not merely a distinguished science, it was also relevant and capable of drawing the boldest parallels.

Social anthropology thus gradually became less confined to the study of the primitive condition, and persistently led us back to, if not contemporary, at least universal topics. Like a few rare anthropologists before him, Lévi-Strauss was capable of asking general questions, of capturing the interest of researchers in neighboring disciplines, and everyone set about reading and discussing his work. Anthropology was no longer the discipline that studied strange customs of remote peoples; with structuralism, it had something to say about fashion, cooking or table manners. Nothing was insignificant; everything had meaning. In other words, it held out possibilities for new areas of research from an analytical as well as a geographical standpoint. If Lévi-Strauss gave new life to traditional anthropology in France, on the international stage he appeared more as an advocate of the intellectual expansion and renovation of anthropology's traditional subjects of study. And in so doing, he probably paved the way for an anthropology of the contemporary world. If people are the same everywhere, it is no use tramping the remote corners of the world: one might as well stay in one's own village, as he concluded in *Tristes Tropiques*.

–2–

A Source of Influence in France

We can now turn our attention to the work of a few outstanding figures who were undeniably influenced by the work of Claude Lévi-Strauss. I have obviously selected only a few of the most representative examples. It must be said, Lévi-Strauss' thinking had left some trace in almost all anthropological studies by the 1960s. Dichotomous oppositions were suddenly all the rage, and were sometimes something of a caricature. Every aspect of reality was irrevocably reduced to high and low, raw and cooked, or hot and cold. Such almost mechanical applications do not deserve examination. They are indicative of a passing fad, to which structuralism cannot be reduced. It was – and is – more than that.

A Marxist Structuralism

At first sight, a Marxist version of structuralism might seem to be a marriage between the carp and the rabbit, as the French say, for in theory these two systems of thought are opposed in every way. Yet in the 1960s some went down the road opened up by the philosopher Louis Althusser, who in *For Marx* and *Reading "Capital"*, undertook to "structuralize" Marx.[1] It was a bold undertaking indeed, intellectually stimulating and one that met with great success among the younger generations. Althusser became a veritable *maître à penser* and gave Marxist theory a new impetus.

In anthropology it fell to Maurice Godelier to connect structuralism and Marxism. Although he was not a disciple of Althusser, Godelier adopted a conception of Marxism that was relatively close to that of the philosopher, most notably in placing the concept of mode of production at the center of the analysis of social reality.[2] From then on it was a matter of picking a few models and seeing how these fit together within the "social formations". Without really daring to criticize Marx, Godelier affirmed that Marxism was in no way a "vulgar materialism", and he maintained that kinship or religion could play *dominant* roles in some modes of production.[3] Relations of production, Marxism *oblige*, were no longer any more than *determining*, or even "determining in the last instance".

This distinction between domination and determination may seem slightly cryptic today, but it fueled some heated debates at the time. For a long time Godelier maintained that, in "primitive" societies, kinship relations fulfilled the function of relations of production. He seemed to imply that Marx's theory only held for Europe and the industrialized world.[4] In the case of what Godelier continued to call "primitive" societies, Lévi-Strauss' structuralism provided the added ingredient necessary to the analysis.

From a few Marxian texts, Godelier unearthed the concept of "Asian mode of production", designed to illustrate the specificity of certain forms of development and thus to criticize a unilineal view of evolution.[5] This mode of production involved some kind of articulation between a centralized State and "primitive" communities. Mode of production had become "structuralized": it formed a system of relations between infrastructure and superstructure. It is not certain that it is still necessary to expand on these works, which now seem to have lost much of their interest. Godelier's writing often boils down to an exegesis of Marx's texts in a jargon laced with structuralist terminology. One may even wonder whether Godelier's structuralism was not a way of paying tribute to the fashions of the time and distancing himself from a certain Marxist orthodoxy. Despite a few abstruse texts, which some may have found brilliant, this linking of Marxism and structuralism did not amount to much more than a gloss.

The idea according to which myths are "an illusory representation of Man and the world"[6] is closer to an Althusserian conception of the ideology than to Lévi-Strauss' analyses, which, to my knowledge, say nothing of the kind. Godelier's structuralism no doubt came down to a view of the social as being governed by hidden forces outside the conscious awareness of the actors. Such a broad conception of culture enabled him to reconcile Marx and Lévi-Strauss, but at such a general level that it would have been possible to do the same with most sociologists.[7]

Not much now remains of what the English called "structural Marxism". This decline probably has both political and historical reasons, but it also has to do with the somewhat hermetic character of the theoretical discussions of the time. In social anthropology, Claude Meillassoux's brand of Marxism seems to me to have been far more productive, so that it has better withstood the test of time and has not become wholly irrelevant.[8]

Kinship or Formalism

It is doubtless no accident that Lévi-Strauss rarely ventured into experimental avenues of inquiry, and that he left it to his disciples to develop the more debatable aspects of his work. It was Françoise Héritier, his former student and successor at the Collège de France, who undertook a formalization of social life and particularly of marriage. In a book intended to pursue the master's project on "complex systems of kinship", she was not afraid to say that "the computer has become the indispensable means to find out how marriage really works in societies".[9] Her aim was to bring to light the "fundamental laws of kinship" resting on the fact that "all human societies operate on the basis of the same irrefutable material, which has a finite number of basic configurations".[10] According to Héritier, structures are not conscious models, and the analysis must reveal a mode of reality that transcends lived experience, a world made up of formal rules and models that are the same for everyone.

Much of her work has been devoted to what she terms "semi-complex alliance systems", a phrase that describes societies which have no positive marriage rule but many prohibitions. Whereas Lévi-Strauss had given only limited importance to kinship terminologies, Héritier regards them as crucial. From a structuralist standpoint nomenclatures are a kind of language, which seems to exist independently of the speakers, thus making it possible to attain so-called deep, non-conscious realities. If Héritier is to be believed, kinship among the Samos of Burkina Faso is based on an "Omaha-type" kinship terminology, so named for a Sioux tribe of American Indians. These terminologies present some particularities – like the assimilation of the father to the father's sister's son – which have long intrigued anthropologists, in particular because the same kin term is used to designate persons in different generations.

At this stage it is interesting to note that Omaha terminologies have been studied as realities *sui generis*, well suited to revealing the very foundations of marriage and society. In the anthropological debates and controversies, marriage had become no longer a practice uniting human beings, but a set of rules and taboos, a sort of formal logic. No more need even to question the actors in order to understand their social life, all one had to do was to look at their "jural" system. If actual practice contradicted the rules, other rules were invoked: whereas the logic of the Samos system should rule out repetition of marriages, in fact 75 per cent of marriages take place within the same village, and Héritier is obliged to call on new rules to explain this paradox.[11] Likewise she uses a single terminological equation as the basis for drawing general conclusions about gender relations among the Omaha: if the aunt, female cousin and niece are called "daughter" by the Omaha, it is because, in their society, women are reduced to an inferior category, and this would therefore be an outcome of male domination. In this disembodied sociology, no one goes to the trouble of looking at reality to see if women really are oppressed. Are linguistic practices enough to account for reality and the way social actors behave?

There is no need to spend more time on this work, which was of an experimental nature, an intellectual game played by certain anthropologists and which did not yield the hoped-for results for the simple reason that institutions as rich as marriage cannot be reduced to formal rules. It took the full force of the structuralist fad, sometimes amounting to blindness, not to see what was perfectly clear.

In her most recent work, Héritier has abandoned such formalism and turned to a "softer" and at the same time more convincing version of structuralism. She does not hesitate to step back from Lévi-Strauss. In *Two Sisters and Their Mother,*[12] for instance, she turns her attention to a problem that is original and fascinating: she observes in effect that, in many societies, the incest prohibition applies not only to consanguines, but also to a whole series of affines who are in no way related by blood: for example, intercourse between a man and his wife's sister, his brother's wife or his wife's daughter. This kind of prohibition is found in all parts of the world and at every point in time. It thus poses a veritable anthropological problem: why forbid sexual commerce with persons who are in no way related by blood? Furthermore, why are these prohibitions found more or less all over the world. According to Héritier, these prohibitions, which she calls "prohibitions of the second kind" are not an oddity. If that were the case, they would not be so widespread. On the contrary, they must be regarded as expressions of a basic law of the human mind, namely that same and different must be kept in balance. All human societies have categories of same and different that are conceived in terms of the body and its humors: these principles form a logical substratum that serves as a template for numerous social practices.[13] Although she is still a structuralist, Héritier nonetheless distances herself from

Lévi-Strauss' theory of incest, which, being based on exchange, does not account for incest of the second kind.[14]

She therefore advances a new theory of the incest taboo, in which the prohibition derives from that fundamental feature of the human mind which perpetually strives to maintain a balance between identity and difference. There is a "logical substratum on which ritualizations, prescriptions, and separations are established in all societies".[15] Hot and cold, male and female, dry and wet, light and dark must be kept in balance, and all societies play with these values. No need here to sum up the argumentation of *Two Sisters and Their Mother*. The author has undeniably put her finger on an interesting phenomenon (a particular form of incest). By the same token, the importance of the opposition between same and different seems to be an important operating mechanism of the human mind. But when it comes to saying it is the cause of the incest prohibition, the demonstration may not be altogether convincing. Nevertheless after having engaged in a fairly unproductive analysis of kinship, Françoise Héritier has proven that there is still some life left in structuralism, even if her version is less and less orthodox and no longer all that different from Radcliffe-Brown's structural-functionalism.

Structuralism in India

To be sure, Louis Dumont cannot legitimately be called a disciple of Lévi-Strauss; he is inarguably much more than that. Nevertheless, his work, at least the part that concerns India, is indeed marked by structuralism. True enough, the structuralism in Dumont's case made a detour through Great Britain and, at certain times, echoes the socio-structuralism of Evans-Pritchard, who was Dumont's colleague at Oxford. Unlike Lévi-Strauss, Dumont was also a great ethnographer, and his work bears the stamp of British empiricism. But he is unfailingly French in one respect: his propensity for theorization and generalization. Dumont combined a global reflection with solid fieldwork, and it is doubtless no accident that, as an anthropologist, he was to wield considerable influence in the Anglo-Saxon world. Dumontian structuralism never cuts itself off from empirical realities; and it was in his capacity as an Indian specialist that Dumont would develop his ideas.

One does not find what could be called a methodological reflection in Dumont's work. Or at least it is never set out as such in his writings. One of his merits was indisputably his capacity to render certain theoretical principles operational; and he thereby set a sort of empirical stamp of approval on structuralism. India became a laboratory in which to demonstrate that his method had a certain relevance. Some will argue that, this being the case, one can question the truly structuralist character of Dumont's studies. These do indeed seem far divorced from a certain theoretical orthodoxy, but has such a thing in fact ever existed? Lévi-Strauss himself was far from deploring Dumont's work, in which he recognized a certain kinship with his own.

Dumont's structuralism took a variety of forms. The first traces can be seen in his work on kinship and kin terms among the Dravidian groups of South India. In a brilliant little book entitled *Dravidien et Kariera*, Dumont compares Lévi-Strauss' analyses with South Indian realities. He intends to show the coherency of their social institutions, and goes back to Lévi-Strauss' thesis that alliance is based on cross-cousin marriage: each marriage, oriented as a gift, is part of the overall network of a family's alliances.[16] In passing, let us note that Dumont seems to be drawn to Lévi-Strauss because of the latter's attachment to Mauss' theory. In the same line, the vocabulary of kinship is interpreted as an "expression of marriage", therefore reflecting social practice. The terminology contains alliance, Dumont writes,[17] and, in the final analysis, alliance expresses the exchange rule underlying social life as a whole.

In his studies on caste, structuralism would take on another dimension. He set out to show, first of all, that the caste system is a "structural system", and that what goes on inside the caste is no different from what goes on outside. The same logic therefore permeates all social relations. This conception is not far from the British school of structural-functionalism, and more particularly from Evans-Pritchard, who in the same order of ideas described the Nuer as a "segmentary" society.[18] Yet Dumont did not stop there, but went on to say, first of all, that the social sphere should be understood as a system of relations: "In the caste society, nothing is true by nature and everything by situation, there are no essences but only relations. To say caste is to say structure. This is the origin of the familiar impossibility of universal judgements in India: as long as one considers particular objects – instead of relations – no consistency, no principle can be found."[19] In the second place, he would consider that caste was the expression of what he called ideology, in other words a system of thought. It is the realization of a way of thinking. The Indian way of thinking is altogether typical of the tendency to dichotomize that is a particular feature of the human mind. In India this dualism would take a religious form in the opposition between pure and impure.

Unlike Lévi-Strauss, Dumont applied his structuralism to a concrete society, India, thus making the theory more operational. Dumont began by regarding India as "one". Behind an apparent diversity, he advised looking for the true foundations of this society and thus going beyond the differences between North and South, tribe and caste, great and little traditions. It was therefore religious ideology, and principally the opposition between pure and impure, that founded the social system as a whole. India's specificity lay in what Dumont called the dissociation of status and power: in India, power or the political are subordinated to ritual status. Another of Dumont's fundamental ideas revived one of sociology's old themes, namely the opposition between holism and individualism. According to Dumont, caste, the key feature of Indian society, is omnipresent and obliterates every other reality. Indian civilization is characterized by the predominance of a hierarchical thought and a holistic ideology; by contrast, contemporary Western society seems dominated by egalitarian values and individualism.

Dumont's work sparked an effervescence among Indian anthropologists. And yet all of the hypotheses he advanced, whether they concern the dissociation of status and power, the religious foundations of civilization, the non-temporal character of "systems", the opposition between holism and individualism or the oneness of India, are seriously in question today.[20]

–3–

Anglo-Saxon Anthropology

It was to the enthusiasm of two influential figures that Lévi-Strauss' thought owes its entry into British anthropology. Rodney Needham at Oxford and Edmund Leach at Cambridge became the translators, both properly and figuratively, of his work in spite of it being a radical departure from Malinowskian empiricism. Even though the British were accustomed to theoretical input from France, Lévi-Strauss' work attained such a degree of abstraction that it took the verve of an Edmund Leach to overcome a circumspection widely known to be an almost natural trait of the British. But he was unable to dissipate all reticence, far from it, and in what at times came to look like a *cause nationale* many British anthropologists were not afraid to criticize Lévi-Strauss, on occasion in an almost insulting fashion.[21] However these reservations were nothing compared to the enthusiasm his work ultimately aroused. Of course a certain critical view would be kept in reserve, but Lévi-Strauss became unquestionably a *maître à penser* in social anthropology; a remarkable fact in a discipline more inclined to a certain intellectual skepticism. Structuralists of strict observance were a scarce commodity, to be sure, but Lévi-Strauss' influence was all the greater for having slipped in everywhere, and structuralism sparked new debates.

Alliance Theory

In the early 1960s Rodney Needham translated certain texts by Lévi-Strauss into English and became a self-styled and ardent defender of the French theoretician. Surprisingly Britain's enthusiasm for Lévistraussian structuralism was accompanied by an almost visceral rejection of Radcliffe-Brown's structural-functionalism. Needham carried an obsessive grudge against the latter, while Leach made his "admiration" for Lévi-Strauss the astonishing corollary of a scorn for Radcliffe-Brown.[22] Structuralism, Kuper comments, had the power of a prophetic movement, and its followers were convinced of belonging to a secret society "of the seeing in a world of the blind."[23]

Structuralism provided a way out of the theoretical impasse in which "descent theory", which considered modes of descent reckoning as crucial social features, found itself. Across the Channel, *The Elementary Structures of Kinship* was seen as a radical critique of descent theory. It confirmed Mauss' hypothesis about the universality of exchange as founding social ties and received the name of "alliance theory". The social rule of cross-cousin marriage was regarded as the expression of the individual's integration in a system that is greater than him or herself and independent of individual will.

When the American anthropologist David Schneider challenged this purely sociological and almost mechanical reading of cross-cousin marriage, Needham replied by publishing a small book, *Structure and Sentiment*, intended as a defense of the French anthropologist. As discussed, Needham remarked in passing that Lévi-Strauss used the terms "prescription" and "preference" without distinction, but that in reality Lévi-Strauss' theory applied only to prescriptive systems. In the second edition of *The Elementary Structures*, Lévi-Strauss replied to Needham, affirming that this apparent confusion was not really one at all, since it reflected the discrepancy between the model and reality. Needham found this clarification intolerable and thereafter devoted the bulk of his writing to criticism of Lévi-Strauss' work. He was overcome by a sort of philosophical skepticism and subsequently published almost nothing that was not of a polemical nature.[24]

Edmund Leach

In Cambridge, Edmund Leach sided against his colleagues, notably Goody and Fortes, in defending the positions of Lévi-Strauss. He took it upon himself to write a short work devoted to Lévi-Strauss, which was actually a quite remarkable overview.[25] Leach steered clear of orthodox structuralism, which would have forced him to forsake the empirical premises of British anthropology, but he did start using a structuralist language, looked into topics dear to Lévi-Strauss and discussed the latter's merits. Leach was more than just a disciple: he was capable of being at once critical and creative. Although he was clearly more positive than Needham, he was nonetheless polemical, some would say provocative.

For Leach, structuralism was first and foremost a quest for meaning and above all for hidden meaning. It obliged the analysis to delve beyond the empirical data in search of deeper realities: Lévi-Strauss' thought attempts to show that there is a logical order behind the most uncompromising ethnographic data.[26] There is an actual language of myth, he writes, that the analyst has to discover.

Leach ventured some analyses in this sense. He tried, for example, to show that there was a correspondence between the abusive use of animal names and marriage categories. According to this theory, animals are classified by edibility, and this classification overlaps that of human sexual classifications: domesticated animals are strongly forbidden and in this resemble sisters, who cannot be "consumed" sexually. Farm animals can be consumed, especially when they are young, and thus are like remote kin, whom one can marry in certain circumstances. Animals of the field resemble neighbors, who are at once outsiders and friends, while wild animals are like strangers, with whom one has no relations. There would thus be a connection between non-edibility and sexual access. That is why many insults involve the names of familiar animals, which are often named in simple, even one-syllable terms (dog, cat, pig, etc.). Terms of insult are therefore the expression of an incestuous desire, a means of violating sexual prohibitions.[27]

Such exercises may have been appealing, but they do not stand up to analysis. In the search for hidden meanings, the primary meaning was overlooked, namely that an animal is associated with certain qualities which are, rightly or wrongly, ascribed to it by common sense: a "pig" is first of all a dirty person.[28] Even if there is hidden meaning somewhere, it is not necessarily everywhere. In the preface to his famous *Political Systems of Highland Burma*, Leach himself recognizes that his tendency to look for logics of order was often an illusory pursuit.[29] Later, it is true, he carried Lévi-Strauss' ideas to extremes, claiming that society had to be considered in a mathematical fashion.[30]

While he was often disconcerting, Leach was nevertheless a spokesman for structuralism in Great Britain, and he himself acknowledged that his debt to Lévi-Strauss could be seen throughout his work.[31]

Purity and Danger

It can be said that Lévi-Strauss' ideas were dragged in, to varying degrees, more or less everywhere, even if it was sometimes in a mechanical or caricatural fashion, as in the quest for binary oppositions, which became an almost mandatory exercise. To be sure, British anthropologists always kept a certain critical distance, but the neo-structuralist movement was nevertheless present. Even anthropologists such as Victor Turner, although a product of the Manchester school, which cannot be said to be close to the structuralists, proposed a reading of Ndembu rites "in the manner of Lévi-Strauss".[32] His interest in rituals and their symbolic interpretation clearly shows Lévi-Strauss' influence on a certain conception of anthropology. Thus he reduces the *isoma* ritual to a series of basic oppositions that are a kind of "non-verbal language".[33]

Yet, while acknowledging his debt to the Lévi-Strauss of *The Savage Mind*,[34] Turner stresses the danger of reducing all dyads to one and of believing that the male/female opposition can be reduced to high/low, or superior/inferior in all circumstances. He speaks, for instance, of polysemy and of the "multivocal character" of symbols, which can have different meanings depending on the context.

Turner's case is typical of the influence Lévi-Strauss exerted on British anthropology. Some of the most respected anthropologists gave his work a new dimension. The case of Mary Douglas, however, is more symptomatic of what has been described as the "neo-structuralist" movement. Some have underscored Evans-Pritchard's influence on Douglas, who was his student and acknowledged him as her mentor. But Lévi-Strauss seems to me to have left just as deep a mark, even if it is minimized by Douglas' biographer.[35]

It is true that, in a collective volume devoted to Lévistraussian analysis of myth, Douglas had harsh words for the reductionist aspect of structuralism, which was incapable of viewing myth as an artistic production.[36] In reality she proved to be something of a radical, rejecting the idea of the inversion of reality or the absence of ambiguity in myth interpretation. But she also testified to the care with which she had read the work of the French anthropologist. Thus the imprint (or was it merely a trace?) of the latter can be seen in her best-known book *Purity and Danger*, which also bears witness to the importance of French sociology (notably Durkheim and Mauss) in the foundation of British anthropology.

We thus find in Douglas the same set of influences as in Dumont. Douglas rejects the idea of a cultural materialism according to which ritual prohibitions concerning impurity were the result of preoccupations with hygiene. Filth, she says, is first of all something that is out of place; it is not an isolated phenomenon, and it must be understood as part of a system.[37] Culture is thus perceived as providing the individual with basic categories. The impure therefore can be conceived only with reference to the pure; it is disorder that permits order. Pollution is a power whereby the structure is supposed to protect itself.[38] Douglas shows her Durkheimian side when she presents the preservation of social solidarity as the goal of religious institutions. Pollution is a kind of punishment for violations of the social order from within.[39] Her interest in classifications and their importance for our perception of the world also shows the tie that links Douglas to the French school and which caused Alain Caillé to say that she should be regarded as "Maussian".[40] Indeed Mauss appears to be the common denominator of most of the authors discussed here.

In later studies, Douglas followed up the idea that culture stems from a series of symbols embedded in a structural system.

Culture and Practical Reason

The United States was no doubt less permeable to the ideas and theories of Lévi-Strauss. Of course his work was discussed there as it was throughout the world, but fewer intellectuals espoused his ideas or relayed them. The country that invented culturalism seemed naturally resistant to the idea that the logic of symbolism is a product of the human mind. Marshall Sahlins, who studied and lived in Paris from 1967 to 1969, was no doubt the most successful in making the transition between the French way of thinking and American anthropology. Having first been influenced by "structural Marxism" and neo-evolutionism, Sahlins published *Culture and Practical Reason*,[41] an essay that could be seen as his theoretical program.[42]

The work begins with a radical critique of Marxism, which is incapable of understanding the foundations of the "tribal society". Structuralism takes a step in this direction, but in turn proves to be unable to grasp change: nevertheless, as Sahlins says, structure is the beginning of historical wisdom. At the same time, he does not reject American culturalism and goes on to combine structural analysis with a form of cultural relativism in which things exist for people only through the meaning they give them.[43] For example, each culture decides what is edible and what is not. When all is said and done, Sahlins is no doubt closer to Geertz than to Lévi-Strauss. Both American anthropologists were of course fascinated by the French anthropologist, but they could not bring themselves to break through the boundaries between "them" and "us", and above all, cultural diversity remained the cardinal rule of all anthropology.

Notes

1. L. Althusser, *Pour Marx*, Paris, Maspéro, 1965; L. Althusser and E. Balibar, *Lire le capital*, Paris, Maspéro, 1968.
2. M. Godelier, "Preface", to Marx and Engels, *Sur les sociétés précapitalistes: textes choisis*, Paris, Editions sociales, 1973, p. 141.
3. M. Godelier, *Horizons, trajets marxistes en anthropologie*, Paris, Maspéro, 1973, pp. 333 and 339. English edition: *Perspectives in Marxist Anthropology*, translated by Robert Brain, Cambridge: Cambridge University Press, 1977.
4. Ibid., p. 60.
5. M. Godelier, "La Notion de 'mode de production asiatique' et les schémas marxistes d'évolution des sociétés", in J. Suret-Canale (ed.), *Sur le "mode de production asiatique"*, Paris, Edition sociales, 1974, pp. 47–100.
6. M. Godelier, *Perspectives in Marxist Anthropology*, translated by Robert Brain, Cambridge, Cambridge University Press, 1977.
7. M. Bloch, *Marxism and Anthropology*, Oxford, Oxford University Press, 1983, p. 167.
8. C. Meillassoux, *Maidens, Meal and Money: Capitalism and the Domestic Mode of Production*, Cambridge, Cambridge University Press, 1981.

9. F. Héritier, *L'Exercice de la parenté*, Paris, Gallimard, 1981, p. 9.
10. Ibid., p. 161.
11. F. Héritier, "L'Ordinateur et l'étude du fonctionnement matrimonial d'un système omaha", in Marc Augé (ed.), *Les Domaines de la parenté*, Paris, Maspero, 1975, p. 103.
12. F. Héritier, *Two Sisters and Their Mother: The Anthropology of Incest*, translated by Jeanine Herman, New York, Zone Books, 1999.
13. F. Héritier, *Les Deux soeurs et leur mère: anthropologie de l'inceste*, Paris, Odile Jacob, 1994, p. 15.
14. Héritier, *Les Deux soeurs et leur mère*, p. 23.
15. Héritier, *Two Sisters and Their Mother*, p. 213.
16. L. Dumont, *Dravidien et Kariera: l'alliance du mariage dans l'Inde du Sud et en Australie*, Paris, Mouton, 1975, p. 63.
17. Ibid., p. 97.
18. E. E. Evans-Pritchard, *The Nuer: A Description of the Modes of Livelihood and Political Institutions of a Nilotic People*, Oxford, Clarendon Press, 1940.
19. L. Dumont, "A Structural Definition of a Folk Deity of Tamil Nad: Aiyanar the Lord", pp. 20–32, in Louis Dumont, *Religion, Politics and History in India*, Paris, Mouton, 1970, p. 29.
20. For an overview of these critiques, see Robert Deliège, "L'Inde de Louis Dumont", in Paul Servais (ed.), *Individu et communauté: une confrontation Orient–Occident*, Louvain-la-Neuve, Academia-Bruylant, 2000, pp. 233–43.
21. For a recent example, see A. Campbell, "Tricky Tropes: Styles of the Popular and the Pompous", in Jeremy McClancy and Christian McDonaugh (eds), *Popularizing Anthropology*, London, Routledge, 1996, pp. 58–82.
22. E. Leach, *Rethinking Anthropology*, London, Athlone Press, 1961, p. 2.
23. A. Kuper, *Anthropology and Anthropologists: The Modern*

British School, London, Routledge and Kegan Paul, 1983, p. 169.
24. A. Kuper, *The Invention of Primitive Society: Transformations of an Illusion*, London, Routledge, 1988, p. 228.
25. E. Leach, *Lévi-Strauss*, London, Fontana, 1970.
26. E. Leach (ed.), *The Structural Study of Myth and Totemism*, London, Tavistock, 1967, p. xii.
27. E. Leach, "Anthropological Aspects of Language: Animal Categories and Verbal Abuse", in Eric H. Lenneberg (ed.), *New Directions in the Study of Language*, Cambridge, MA, MIT Press, 1964, pp. 23–63.
28. J. Halverson, "Animal Categories and Terms of Abuse", *Man (NS)*, II, 1976 pp. 505–16.
29. E. Leach, *Political Systems of Highland Burma: A Study of Kachin Social Structure*, London, Athlone Press, 1964, p. xii.
30. Leach, *Rethinking Anthropology*, p. 7.
31. Leach, *Rethinking Anthropology*, p. vi.
32. V. Turner, *The Ritual Process: Structure and Anti-Structure*, London, Routledge and Kegan Paul, 1969, p. 106 (refers to French translation).
33. Turner, *The Ritual Process*, p. 45 (refers to French translation).
34. Turner, *The Ritual Process*, p. 47 (refers to French translation).
35. R. Fardon, *Mary Douglas: An Intellectual Biography*, London, Routledge, 1999.
36. M. Douglas, "The Meaning of Myth", in Leach (ed.), *The Structural Study of Myth and Totemism*, p. 65.
37. M. Douglas, *Purity and Danger: An Analysis of Concepts of Pollution and Taboo*, London, Routledge, 1984, p. 36.
38. Ibid., p. 114.
39. Ibid., p. 134.
40. A. Caillé, "Avant-propos", in Mary Douglas, *Comment pensent les institutions?*, Paris, La Découverte, 1999, p. 7; translated from the English: *How Institutions Think*, New

York, Syracuse University Press, 1986.

41. M. Sahlins, *Culture and Practical Reason*, Chicago, University of Chicago Press, 1976.
42. A. Kuper, *Culture: The Anthropologist's Account*, Cambridge, MA, Harvard University Press, 1999, p. 164.
43. Sahlins, *Culture and Practical Reason*, p. 215 (refers to French translation).

Conclusion

In the social sciences there is a paradox whereby the classic theories also appear to be anachronistic. They recall those ancient monuments that, having lost their function, exist merely as testimonies to a bygone era. This could certainly be the case of the work of Claude Lévi-Strauss, and all the more because his taste for abstraction systematically creates a great distance between him and concrete reality of any kind. Moreover it would be useless to attempt to find a method for apprehending such reality. Yet we have just seen that, like all great bodies of work, his continues to inspire numerous authors, and I believe this will continue to be the case for a long time to come, for the treasure house of his thought is far from being exhausted.

Throughout these pages, we have looked at his work from an anthropological standpoint. In some regards, however, this is not the best angle of approach, and, if a general critique of his writings were required, I would say that they are more of a philosophy or a metaphysics than a sociological theory. His work and his analyses had so little that was operational about them; they were so recalcitrant to any reality, that they are often a disappointment to students or to young anthropologists who, on their first time in the field, are confronted with contingencies of an altogether different nature. We must therefore not ask of this work what it cannot give. Its interest and its richness lie more in specific aspects than in the work as a whole. To take just one example, certain features of his myth analyses are truly fascinating and have changed our approach to mythology considerably (comparison of the different versions, search for internal oppositions, discovery of an underlying logic ...). At the same time, the "general science" of mythology and the conclusions the author invites us to draw are so extreme that they can sometimes seem far fetched. If myths are trying to say something, the key to their explanation should be sought closer to home. This was my sentiment the first time I collected myths among the Untouchables in South India. To interpret them following Lévi-Strauss to the letter would have been to distort them completely; but at the same time his ingenious intuition and his fecundity invariably lent a certain coloring to my analyses. The different variations had to be compared and an underlying structure sought.

The Elementary Structures of Kinship inspires a similar fascination and numbers among those works that do not leave the reader unchanged. Moreover this is true of many of Lévi-Strauss' books, which have stamped their mark on all of the social sciences in the second half of the twentieth century. Of course today the crest of the wave has passed, and anthropology in particular has turned to other avenues of investigation, more historical and pragmatic. But the fact is that it perhaps now lacks that visionary aspect which sets off debate, criticism, enthusiasm and intellectual effervescence.

In the end, Lévi-Strauss seems to be as much an artist as a scholar. His taste for order, rigor and analysis is unfailingly associated throughout his work with a certain sense of creativity and invention. In a way it can be said that he has made us dream as much as he has made us think. He reminds us that social anthropology can be something more than a simple collection of facts, and that is the lesson Leach retains: "It is still possible to base speculative generalizations on Malinowski's facts, and I believe that speculative generalization, even if it often proves wrong, is very well worth while."[1]

Notes

1. E. Leach, *Rethinking Anthropology*, London, University of London, Athlone Press, 1961, p. 27.

Glossary

Abreaction. Emotional discharge whereby the subject is liberated from the feelings attached to a traumatic experience.

Anthropology. Originally the study of primitive societies, today extending to complex societies as well. It is also called "social anthropology" or "cultural anthropology", and used to be known as ethnology. Ethnography is the first stage of research in anthropology; it consists in the collection of data and information.

Avuncular relation. The relation between mother's brother and sister's son.

Cross cousins. Cousins who are children of a brother *and* a sister, as opposed to parallel cousins, who are children of two brothers *or* two sisters.

Descent. The principle governing the transmission of kin ties. Patrilineal descent is reckoned from father to son, matrilineal descent, from mother's brother to sister's son.

Determinism. The scientific principle according to which a phenomenon cannot occur without specific conditions.

Diachrony. A perspective that stresses time depth and change.

Empiricism. The idea or doctrine that knowledge derives from experience.

Exchange. In Mauss' perspective, exchange is the very basis of the social bond. It derives from gift-giving, which is the synthetic form of exchange, comprising the obligations to give, to receive and to give in return.

Exogamy. Marriage outside a given group. Opposite of endogamy in which marriage is within a given group.

Exoticism. The taste for the practices, customs and artistic expressions of remote peoples.

Functionalism. A theory according to which all social institutions contribute to the maintenance of society. It was very influential in British anthropology and linked to the method of participant observation.

Kinship. The set of relations resulting from alliance (marriage) and consanguinity.

Myths. The founding tales that the members of a society pass on from one generation to the next.

Participant observation. A technique of anthropological fieldwork (or ethnography) that consists of the immersion of the researcher into the daily life of the people studied.

Preferential marriage. Marriage between cross cousins.

Rationalism. The doctrine that holds that knowledge can be derived from reason. In anthropology it is often opposed to empiricism and relativism.

Relativism. The doctrine or view that opposes the idea of human universals and values. In anthropology it is often opposed to ethnocentrism.

Romanticism. A movement, particularly in the arts, that places value on the self, sensitivity, reverie and exaltation.

Shaman. Siberian ecstatic priest. By extension any trance specialist who acts as a mediator between this world and a world beyond.

Social structure. All those relations that bind together the individuals in a social group.

Structural-functionalism. Theory centered on the study of social structure. In social anthropology it has been associated with the work of Radcliffe-Brown; it privileged both a synchronic and sociological perspective.

Structuralism. A movement in the human sciences patterned on a linguistic model that attempts to reduce social phenomena to a formal set of relations.

Structure. A whole made up of interrelated elements such that each element depends on the others to create a set of relations. Modification of any one element leads to the modification of all the others.

Symbolic classification. The ways things are classified into categories of the mind.

Terminology of kinship. The set of terms used in a language to designate persons related by blood and by marriage.

Totems. An Ojibwa Indian term designating the animals and plants that act as symbols for social groups.

Unconscious. In psychoanalysis, the unconscious denotes the conflictual content buried in the mind that determines our behavior.

Uxorilocal. A form of postmarital residence in which the couple moves into the woman's house. Opposite of virilocal in which the couple moves into the man's house.

Selected Bibliography

Principal Works by Claude Lévi-Strauss

Anthropology and Myth: Lectures, 1951–1982, translated by Roy Willis, Oxford, Blackwell, 1987; original title: *Paroles données*, Paris, Plon, 1984.

Conversations with Claude Lévi-Strauss, edited by Georges Charbonnier, translated by John and Doreen Weightman, London, Cape, 1969; original title: *Entretiens avec Claude Lévi-Strauss par Georges Charbonnier*, Paris, Plon/Julliard, 1961.

Conversations with Claude Lévi-Strauss, with Didier Eribon, translated by Paula Wissing, Chicago, University of Chicago Press, 1991; original title: *De près et de loin: entretiens avec Didier Eribon*, Paris, Odile Jacob, 1988.

Des symboles et leurs doubles, Paris, Plon, 1989.

The Elementary Structures of Kinship, translated by James Harle Bell, John Richard von Sturmer and Rodney Needham, Boston, Beacon Press, 1969; original title: *Les Structures élémentaires de la parenté*, Paris, Presses Universitaires de France, 1949 (new revised edition, Paris, Mouton, 1967).

From Honey to Ashes, Introduction to a Science of Mythology, volume 2, translated by John and Doreen Weightman, Chicago, University of Chicago Press, 1983; original title: *Mythologiques II, Du miel aux cendres*, Paris, Plon, 1967.

Introduction to the Work of Marcel Mauss, translated by Felicity Baker, London, Routledge and Kegan Paul, 1987; original title: "Introduction à l'œuvre de Marcel Mauss", in

Marcel Mauss, *Sociologie et anthropologie,* Paris, Presses Universitaires de France, 1950, pp. ix–l.

The Jealous Potter, translated by Bénédicte Chorier, Chicago, University of Chicago Press, 1988; original title: *La Potière jalouse*, Paris, Plon, 1985.

The Naked Man, *Introduction to a Science of Mythology*, volume 4, translated by John and Doreen Weightman, Chicago, University of Chicago Press, 1990; original title: *Mythologiques IV, L'Homme nu*, Paris, Plon, 1971.

The Origin of Table Manners, *Introduction to a Science of Mythology*, volume 3, translated by John and Doreen Weightman, Chicago, University of Chicago Press, 1990; original title: *Mythologiques III, L'Origine des manières de table*, Paris, Plon, 1968.

Race and History, Paris, Unesco, 1952; original title: *Race et histoire*, Paris, Unesco, 1952 (new edition, Paris, Gonthier, 1975).

The Raw and the Cooked, Introduction to a Science of Mythology, volume 1, translated by John and Doreen Weightman, New York, Penguin, 1986; original title: *Mythologiques I, Le Cru et le cuit*, Paris, Plon, 1964.

The Savage Mind, Chicago, University of Chicago Press, 1969 [no translator mentioned]; original title: *La Pensée sauvage*, Paris, Plon, 1962.

The Story of Lynx, translated by Catherine Tihany, Chicago, University of Chicago Press, 1995; original title: *Histoires de lynx*, Paris, Plon, 1991.

Structural Anthropology, translated by Claire Jacobson and Brooke Grundfest Schoepf, New York, Basic Books, 1963; original title: *Anthropologie structurale*, Paris, Plon, 1958.

Structural Anthropology II, translated by Monique Layton, London, Allen Lane, 1977; original title: *Anthropologie structurale deux*, Paris, Plon, 1973.

Totemism, translated by Rodney Needham, London, Penguin, 1969; original title: *Le Totémisme aujourd'hui*, Paris, Presses Universitaires de France, 1962.

Tristes Tropiques, translated by John and Doreen Weightman, New York, Penguin, 1992; original title: *Tristes tropiques*, Paris, Plon, 1955.

The View from Afar, translated by Joachim Neugroschel and Phoebe Hoss, Chicago, University of Chicago Press, 1992; original title: *Le Regard éloigné*, Paris, Plon, 1983.

The Way of the Masks, translated by Sylvia Modelski, Seattle, University of Washington Press, c1982; original title: *La Voie des masques*, Geneva, Skira, 1975.

Works about Lévi-Strauss

Badcock, C., *Lévi-Strauss: Structuralism and Sociological Theory*, London, Hutchinson, 1975.

Clément, C., *Lévi-Strauss ou la structure et le malheur*, Paris, Seghers, 1970.

Cressant, P., *Lévi-Strauss*, Paris, Editions Universitaires, 1970.

Delfendahl, B., *Le Clair et l'obscur*, Paris, Anthropos, 1973.

Delruelle, E., *Lévi-Strauss et la philosophie*, Brussels, De Boeck, 1989.

Dubuisson, D., *Mythologies du XXe siècle (Dumézil, Lévi Strauss, Eliade)*, Lille, Presses Universitaires de Lille, 1993.

Giovacchini, D. (ed.), *Analyses et réflexions sur Claude Lévi-Strauss: "Tristes tropiques"*, Paris, Ellipses, 1992.

Hénaff, M., *Claude Lévi-Strauss and the Making of Structural Anthropology,* translated by Mary Baker, Minneapolis, University of Minnesota Press, 1998; original title: *Claude Lévi-Strauss*, Paris, Belfond, 1991.

Lapointe, F. and Lapointe, C., *Claude Lévi-Strauss and His Critics: An International Bibliography (1950–1976)*, New York, Garland, 1991.

Leach, E., *Lévi-Strauss*, London, Fontana, 1970.

Leach, E., (ed.), *The Structural Study of Myth and Totemism*, London, Tavistock, 1967.

Lefebvre, H., *Contre l'idéologie structuraliste*, Paris, Le Seuil, 1975.

Makarius, R. and Makarius, L., *Structuralisme ou ethnologie: pour une critique radicale du structuralisme de Lévi-Strauss*, Paris, Anthropos, 1973.

Rossi, I., (ed.), *The Unconscious in Culture: The Structuralism of Claude Lévi-Strauss in Perspective*, New York, Dutton, 1974.

Simonis, Y., *Claude Lévi-Strauss ou la passion de l'inceste*, Paris, Flammarion, 1980.

Sperber, D., *Le Structuralisme en anthropologie*, Paris, Le Seuil, 1968.

Works about Structuralism

Boudon, R., *The Uses of Structuralism*, translated by Michalina Vaughan and introduced by Donald MacRae, London, Heinemann, 1971; original title: *A quoi sert la notion de "structure"? Essai sur la signification de la notion de structure dans les sciences humaines*, Paris, Gallimard, 1968.

Dosse, F., *Histoire du structuralisme*, Paris, La Découverte, 1991, 2 vols.

Fages, J.-B., *Comprendre le structuralisme*, Toulouse, Privat, 1968.

Lefebre, H., *L'Idéologie structuraliste*, Paris, Le Seuil, 1971.

Needham, R., *Structure and Sentiment: A Test Case in Social Anthropology*, Chicago, University of Chicago Press, 1962.

Piaget, J., *Structuralism*, translated by Chaninah Maschler, New York, Basic Books, 1970; original title: *Le Structuralisme*, Paris, Presses Universitaires de France, 1968.

Robey, D., (ed.), *Structuralism: An Introduction*, Oxford, Oxford University Press, 1973.

Viet, J., *Les Méthodes structuralistes dans les sciences sociales*, Paris, Mouton, 1965.

Index

The titles of works by Lévi-Strauss are listed at the end of the entry under his name